A LEGACY IN MOTION:

Celebrating 30 Years of the
Black History 101
Mobile Museum

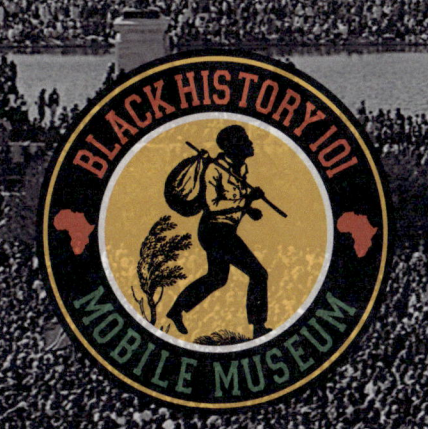

KHALID EL-HAKIM, PH.D.

Educational Fair Use Disclaimer
The images reproduced in this book are included for educational and informational purposes only. They serve to illustrate and enhance the historical and cultural significance of the topics discussed within the text. Under the principles of *Fair Use* as outlined in Section 107 of the U.S. Copyright Act, the use of these images is not intended for commercial exploitation but rather to provide critical commentary, scholarship, and teaching. Every effort has been made to attribute the original creators and sources of these materials accurately. Should any copyright holder feel their work has been improperly utilized, we encourage them to contact us directly.

THE GREATEST PUBLISHING
COPYRIGHT 2024

DETROIT • MIAMI

بِسْمِ ٱللَّهِ ٱلرَّحْمَٰنِ ٱلرَّحِيمِ

ACKNOWLEDGEMENTS

A Legacy in Motion, is the culmination of countless moments, memories, and the unwavering support of those who have been part of my journey. I owe a tremendous debt of gratitude to everyone who has played a role in making this work a reality.

First and foremost, I extend my heartfelt appreciation to my family (my wife Tasleem, daughters: Keisha, BreAna, Monique, Maryam, and Khalilah and my mother), whose love and encouragement have been the foundation of all that I do. Your belief in me has fueled my passion and drive, and your sacrifices have allowed me to pursue this vision.

To the countless educators, activists, and historians who inspired my path. It would take a whole to list your names. I thank you for illuminating the power of history to transform lives. Your contributions to our collective understanding have been a guiding light in this work.

To the Black History 101 Mobile Museum team (Griff, Omari, Victor, and Duminie) you have been instrumental in bringing this vision to life. Your dedication, hard work, and commitment to preserving and sharing our history have made an immeasurable impact.

I also want to acknowledge the individuals and communities who have trusted me with their stories, artifacts, and memories. Your generosity and willingness to share your histories have enriched this project in ways words cannot express.

To my friends, colleagues, and mentors, thank you for challenging me, encouraging me, and holding me accountable to the mission. Your insights and guidance have been invaluable throughout this process.

A special thanks to the many venues, institutions, and educators who have hosted the Black History 101 Mobile Museum over the years. Your openness to learning and teaching history has been a testament to the power of education to bring about change.

Finally, to the reader holding this book in your hands, thank you for your curiosity and commitment to understanding the past to inform our present and shape our future. This work is for you, and I hope it inspires you to carry forward the legacy of those who came before us.

Peace,
Khalid el-Hakim, Ph.D

CELEBRATION
A poem by Abiodun Oyewole of the Last Poets

HIS NAME IS KHALID EL HAKIM PHD
LOVED HIS PEOPLE SO MUCH
HE STUDIED THEM
RESEARCHED THEM
DISCOVERED THEIR GENIUS
WROTE HIS DISSERTATION ABOUT THEM
EARNED A DOCTORATE DEGREE
FOR HIS LOVE FOR HIS PEOPLE
CREATED A MOBILE MUSEUM
TRAVELS ALL OVER THE COUNTRY
WITH ARTIFACTS PICTURES INFORMATION
ABOUT WHAT BLACKS HAVE DONE
IN AMERICA
HE IS A ONE-MAN MOVEMENT
OF BLACK PRIDE
BLACK BRILLIANCE
BLACK LOVE
DON'T NEED NO BLACKBOARD WITH WHITE
CHALK
JUST A SPACE TO PLACE
THE EXAMPLES THE PROOF
THE MEMORABILIA
OF HOW GREAT BLACKS ARE
SO THE WORLD CAN SEE
BE REMINDED
THERE AIN'T NOBODY LIKE US
NOBODY CAN DO THE THINGS WE DO
EVEN WHEN THEY SAY
WE AIN'T NOBODY
KHALID PUT BLACKS ON DISPLAY
MADE EVERY DAY A BLACK DAY
LET YOU KNOW
FROM THE SHACKLES WE WORE
TO THE INVENTIONS WE CREATED
FROM THE BLUES WE SUNG
TO THE JAZZ OF LIBERATION
HOW WE TOOK THE CHAINS
AND CHANGED THE WORLD
HOW WE TOOK THE PAIN
BROUGHT JOY TO EVERYBODY
HE TELLS THE STORY
HE GIVES YOU THE VISUAL
OF THE GOD INSIDE OF US
HIS MOBILE MUSEUM
ALLOWS MALCOLM AND MARCUS
MARTIN AND HARRIET
SOJOURNER AND ROSA PARKS
DR. CLARK AND AMIRI
THE BLACK PANTHERS AND TUPAC
DICK GREGORY AND SONIA SANCHEZ
BLACK POETRY AND BLACK MUSIC
YOU AND ME TO LIVE FOREVER

Abiodun Oyewole (Photo by: Khalid el-Hakim)

TABLE OF CONTENTS

The Beginning	1
From Promise to Purpose:	
The Birth of the Black History 101 Mobile Museum	3
From The Classroom to Exhibiting in Public Spaces	5
When History Speaks: The Voices of Living Legends	8
The Genius of Proof	13
PROFESSOR GRIFF AND THE BLACK HISTORY 101 MOBILE MUSEUM: A JOURNEY OF COLLABORATION	16

Chapter 1
GROUNDBREAKERS & GAME-CHANGERS: REDEFINING EXCELLENCE	20

Chapter 2
RISE UP: ARTIFACTS OF RESISTANCE & LIBERATION	42

Chapter 3
SOUNDWAVES OF CHANGE: THE POWER OF BLACK EXPRESSION	68

Chapter 4
THE ABSURDITY OF WHITENESS: CONFRONTING EVERYDAY RACISM	91

Chapter 5
BEYOND BORDERS: GLOBAL BLACK INFLUENCE	115
30 Years of photographic memories	125
FLYERS	145
AWARDS	152
EPILOGUE	161

THE BEGINNING

My journey into collecting artifacts as a means of teaching history began during my time at Ferris State University, where I enrolled in an Introduction to Sociology class with Dr. David Pilgrim. He was one of only four Black professors I encountered throughout my college and graduate school experience. From the moment I stepped into his classroom, I felt an undeniable connection to him—not only because of our shared cultural heritage but because of his unique ability to teach history using artifacts. His approach sparked something deep within me.

One day, Dr. Pilgrim brought an artifact to class that forever changed how I viewed history. It was a cast-iron bank, grotesquely crafted to resemble a caricatured Black man, with exaggerated red lips, protruding white eyes, and ears that seemed almost cartoonish. The bank's arm held an open hand meant for coins, and with the flip of a lever, the hand would lift the coin into the figure's wide, grinning mouth. On its back were the words, "Little Nigger Bank." I was horrified. I had never seen anything like it in my life.

As the class discussion unfolded, my mind raced back to childhood memories of watching television. Shows like *Tom and Jerry*, *Bugs Bunny*, *The Little Rascals*, and even *Shirley Temple* films came flooding back. I realized how often those racist, blackface images had been right in front of me—yet I had never critically questioned them. In that moment, I was struck by how deficient my education had been. The history I had been taught ignored the brutal ways stereotypes and propaganda were weaponized against Black people. Dr. Pilgrim's method of using artifacts didn't just teach history—it made it impossible to ignore. The physicality of these objects forced us out of our comfort zones, confronting us with the hard truths of our shared past.

One day, Dr. Pilgrim shared that this particular bank was just one example among thousands of products that depicted Black people in dehumanizing ways. I was captivated—and deeply disturbed—by the sheer volume of these artifacts. What was more shocking was realizing that many of these products were not relics of a distant past; their echoes remained alive and palpable in the world around us.

The "Little Nigger Bank" discussion sparked an inquiry in me that still has me asking questions of "how" and "why" when it comes to racism.

Dr. David Pilgrim, Elaine Steele and I at a Black History Month program at Big Rapids High School in 1993.

After that class, I felt compelled to act. I began my own journey of collecting Jim Crow-era artifacts, frequenting antique shops, flea markets, and estate sales. My first artifact came during a spring break trip with college friends to Daytona Beach, Florida. On the way, we stopped at a gas station in Tennessee. What I saw there rattled me to my core: shelves lined with Confederate flags, reproduction figurines of mammies and sambos, and other grotesque stereotypes I had only recently learned about. I was livid—tempted to knock over the displays—but ultimately, I acquired a pocket-sized figurine: a Black boy sitting on a pot, eating a slice of watermelon. That was the first piece in what would become known as the Black History 101 Mobile Museum.

Later, in Daytona Beach, I encountered something even more disturbing. In a souvenir shop selling trinkets and beach gear, I spotted a horrifying glass etching behind the counter: an image of Dr. Martin Luther King Jr. with a target over his face and a bullet hole etched in the glass. Beneath it, the words "Our Dream Came True" were inscribed. The cashier grinned wickedly as I stood frozen in disbelief. That moment was a violation of my humanity, a wound so deep it could not be ignored.

That emptiness, that feeling of profound violation, is something I recognize in the faces of those who walk through the Black History 101 Mobile Museum today. But unlike my experiences in those gas stations and shops, the museum offers something powerful: a chance to confront these artifacts in a space designed for critical dialogue. Dr. Pilgrim's class taught me the transformative power of artifacts in education, and now, I use that same power to spark conversations, challenge perceptions, and inspire action. History, when taught this way, is not just a subject—it's a force for awakening and change.

The artifact that started it all.

This t-shirt has the exact same image that was on the glass etching in the Daytona Beach souvenir shop.

2

FROM PROMISE TO PURPOSE: THE BIRTH OF THE BLACK HISTORY 101 MOBILE MUSEUM

In early 1995, I found myself among over 10,000 Black men gathered at Joe Louis Arena in Detroit, listening to a powerful address by Minister Louis Farrakhan. At that time, I only knew him as the leader of the Nation of Islam, a figure I had encountered through Public Enemy's music and KRS-One's videos. That night, as he spoke about accountability, reconciliation, and responsibility, he issued a call for one million Black men to convene in Washington, D.C., on October 16th for what would be known as the Million Man March.

On that historic day, I was overwhelmed by the significance of the moment standing amongst more than the one million man who were called. It was more than a gathering; it was a collective recommitment to our communities and to each other. As I listened to historical and cultural giants like Stevie Wonder, Rosa Parks, Dr. Dorothy Height, Jesse Jackson, and Maya Angelou speak words of encouragement and empowerment, I felt a profound shift within myself. This wasn't just a day of action—it was a day of transformation.

As I look back on the 30-year journey of the Black History 101 Mobile Museum, I am reminded of how a single moment can alter the trajectory of a life. For me, that moment came on October 16, 1995. Standing there, I made a promise to myself: to use whatever gifts I had to contribute to the collective upliftment of my people and humanity.

The collector in me recognized the importance of preserving that day's history. I purchased buttons, posters, t-shirts, newspapers, and even kept my Metro Subway Card with the date stamped on it. These small artifacts became reminders of a monumental event. However, as the years went by, I noticed how easily this history was being erased. To this day, in my travels across the country, I rarely see the Million Man March mentioned in textbooks, and most students I meet have never heard of it.

Returning to Detroit after the march, I felt a renewed sense of purpose. At the time, I was a young teacher, recently hired as a reading instructor at the Detroit Job Corps, working with students who had often been overlooked or underestimated. I quickly realized that traditional teaching methods weren't enough to engage them. Inspired by the march and my growing collection of artifacts, I began bringing history into the classroom in tangible ways. A single photograph, a vintage magazine, or a record could spark curiosity and ignite meaningful conversations that a textbook never could. These artifacts made history accessible, relatable, and real.

This approach to teaching became a cornerstone of my pedagogy when I transitioned to teaching middle school in the Detroit Public Schools. For 13 years, I used artifacts to connect students to the broader narratives of American history. I watched as their eyes lit up, their questions deepened, and their understanding of the world expanded. These moments were the seeds of what would eventually grow into the Black History 101 Mobile Museum.

Shortly after the Million Man March, I began sharing my collection beyond the classroom. I partnered with Minister Malik Shabazz of the New Marcus Garvey Movement, whose grassroots organization was instrumental in addressing issues like closing crack houses and boycotting businesses that disrespected Black customers. Minister Shabazz graciously gave me space to display my artifacts at several of his meetings, which often featured influential Black scholars and activists such as Dr. Leonard Jeffries, Dell Jones, and Dr. Khallid Muhammad. My first exhibit consisted of just twenty items, but the response was overwhelming. People were surprised to learn the collection was mine, often assuming it came from an institution like the Charles Wright Museum.

Minister Malik Shabazz, Mudd, Thyme (5 ELA), Professor Griff and I

That initial display was transformative. It reinforced my belief that preserving and sharing our history could inspire action and build community. What started as a private passion project—a way to connect my students to history—began to take on a larger purpose.

The Million Man March was the catalyst for this journey. It instilled in me a sense of accountability, unity, and purpose that has guided my life's work. Today, as I reflect on the 30-year journey of the Black History 101 Mobile Museum, I see how that single moment in Washington, D.C., set me on a path I could never have imagined. It was there that I made a promise to use my gifts to uplift my community—a promise that continues to shape my work and my life.

My mother and grandmother attended my first major exhibit at the Detroit Job Corps in February 1997. It was the only time my grandmother experienced the exhibit.

FROM THE CLASSROOM TO EXHIBITING IN PUBLIC SPACES

The Black History 101 Mobile Museum began as a modest collection—a one or two tables of artifacts displayed in classrooms and at local community events. But as the collection grew, so did its reach and impact. I realized that these artifacts had a life beyond the walls of a classroom. They told stories that transcended geography, age, and background. They held the power to ignite conversations and foster connections. And so, the Black History 101 Mobile Museum was born: a traveling exhibit designed to bring these stories to people wherever they were.

Taking this idea on the road wasn't an easy decision. By 2010, I had turned 40, was newly married, and my youngest daughter on the way. Leaving my teaching job with its guaranteed income to pursue the museum full-time was a leap of faith—but it was a calculated risk. I developed a 10-year plan: I would give the museum my all for a decade. If the venture didn't succeed, I would go back to teaching, but not without a backup plan. I committed to earning a graduate degree during that time so I would have something to fall back on.

In 2014, I achieved one of the milestones in that plan by earning my master's degree. That accomplishment not only gave me security but also opened my perspective to the possibility of pursuing a Ph.D. It was the best professional decision I ever made, and I haven't looked back since.

A critical component of the Black History 101 Mobile Museum's success has been the support of a reliable and dedicated team. Two longtime friends, Omari Barksdale and Duminie DePorres, have been integral to this journey, assisting with everything from driving and providing an extra set of eyes to curating and presenting at events. Both friendships were built through shared connections in music—Omari was part of the 3rd Eye Open Poetry Collective, and Duminie was the guitarist for Enemy Squad, a funk band led by Gabe Gonzales, a friend I've known since middle school. In 2007, Omari and Duminie stepped up to help take the museum on the road and have been consistently traveling with me ever since. Last year, Victor Muhammad joined the team, bringing fresh energy and playing a key role in expanding the museum's reach.

As demand for the museum has grown, so has the need to adapt. To meet the increasing requests for exhibits, we've evolved into a multi-team operation. What started as a

Omari, Duminie, longtime collaborator and friend Sharif Liwaru, and I catching up in Vancouver, WA.

Victor Muhammad with Victor Williams and his wife at an exhibit at the Main Library in Grand Rapids, MI.

single group handling all aspects of the museum has transformed into a coordinated effort with multiple teams traveling simultaneously. In January and February, which are particularly busy months due to Martin Luther King Jr. Day and Black History Month, we organize three separate teams, each equipped with a unique exhibit. These teams travel to different parts of the country, ensuring we can engage with schools, universities, libraries, and corporations nationwide.

This approach not only allows us to meet the high demand during peak times but also ensures that the museum's mission of connecting communities to history, identity, and social justice continues to reach as many audiences as possible. By working together, we've been able to expand the museum's reach while maintaining the quality and impact of the experience at every stop.

Over the past 30 years, the museum has visited 43 states and traveled to over 1,000 institutions, including schools, universities, libraries, corporations, and cultural events. From small classrooms to large conferences, it has sparked conversations about history, identity, and social justice. It has become a bridge between the past and the present, connecting audiences to the stories that define us.

But this journey has never been just about the artifacts. The real power of the museum lies in its ability to combine these tangible pieces of history with the voices of those who lived it. Through the inclusion of living legends and historical icons in our storytelling, the museum has become more than a collection—it is a dynamic, interactive experience that brings history to life.

Taking that leap of faith at 40 to give this idea 10 years of my full commitment shaped the course of my life. Earning my master's degree along the way was a turning point that prepared me for new opportunities, including pursuing my Ph.D. The museum's journey from a small classroom collection to a national traveling exhibit has been a testament to the power of planning, resilience, and the enduring importance of preserving and sharing our history.

Omari and Griff engaging students in a conversation after they walked through the exhibit in Tigard, OR.

David Bell takes in the Black History 101 Mobile Museum at the University of Michigan – Ann Arbor.

WHEN HISTORY SPEAKS: THE VOICES OF LIVING LEGENDS

It is one thing to see a historical artifact. It is another to hear from the people who lived the history those artifacts represent. Over the years, the Black History 101 Mobile Museum has had the immense privilege of welcoming living legends to share their stories directly with audiences. These individuals have breathed life into the collection, making the experience deeply personal and unforgettable. People like **The Last Poets**, whose groundbreaking spoken word paved the way for hip-hop, have stood beside artifacts and spoken about their revolutionary beginnings. **Jessica Care Moore**, a cultural icon and poet, has shared her journey in shaping contemporary Black literature. **Sam Greenlee**, whose novel **The Spook Who Sat by the Door** became a cornerstone of revolutionary storytelling, spoke about the intersections of art and activism.

The contributions of **Dee McNeil of The Watts Prophets**, **The Velvelettes**, and **Chairman Fred Hampton, Jr.** have further deepened the museum's offerings, while figures like **Dr. Khalilah Ali** and **Maryam Ali** have shared intimate reflections on the life and legacy of Muhammad Ali. **MC Sha Rock,** hip-hop's first female emcee and a member of The Funky Four + 1, has captivated audiences by recounting her pioneering role in the birth of hip-hop, breaking barriers in a male-dominated industry. Her voice reminds us that women were instrumental in shaping the culture from its inception. **Hayley Marie Norman**, an actor and advocate for representation in media, has brought her unique perspective to the museum's storytelling. Through her work and reflections, she bridges the past and present, highlighting the ongoing struggle for equity and inclusion in Hollywood and beyond.

Ernie Paniccioli, hip-hop's visual historian, has provided audiences with a vivid window into the early days of the movement, while **Paradise Gray of X Clan** has shown how hip-hop continues to serve as a platform for liberation and the importance of archiving the culture. And, of course, the museum has been graced by the presence of Chuck D, a revolutionary voice in hip-hop and social justice.

These voices have elevated the museum from a collection of artifacts to a living archive of Black excellence, resistance, and resilience. Audiences don't just encounter history; they feel it, question it, and connect with it on a deeply emotional level. By integrating these living legends into the fabric of the museum's storytelling, the Black History 101 Mobile Museum ensures that history is not just remembered—it is lived, shared, and carried forward by those who continue to shape it. This aspect of the museum's work has become one of its most unique and transformative offerings, creating an experience that connects people not only to the past but also to the ongoing legacy of those who are making history today.

The Last Poets and I at the Original Hip Hop Shop in Detroit.

With Maryum Ali (eldest daughter of Muhammad Ali) at MSU Denver's MLK Day celebration.

Dee McNeil of The Watts Prophets and I in LA.

The City of Lansing honored MC ShaRock, Professor Griff and I on June 26th naming it Hip Hop Day in celebration of the 50th anniversary of hip hop.

The Velvelettes of Motown Records fame sharing stories with students at Kalamazoo College.

Jessika Murphy of UC-East Bay invited Chairman Fred Hampton, Jr. and I to present at their Black History Month event.

Khalilah Ali (former wife of Muhammad Ali) and I met with General Christopher Gwabin Musa, Chief of Defence Staff of Nigeria.

10

Sam Greenlee, author of The Spook Who Sat by The Door on one of his many visits to Detroit. Sam was a frequent guest speaker with the Black History 101 Mobile Museum.

Ernie Paniccioli, Kenny Muhammad, and I at Kalamazoo College.

Hollywood actor, Hayley Marie Norman was the guest speaker at Northwestern University in Boston.

Long time friend and collaborator Jessica Care Moore and I in Flint showing off our portraits in Ernie Paniccioli's Book Stark: Kiss the Ring.

12

THE GENIUS OF PROOF: A REFLECTION ON FRIENDSHIP, LEGACY, AND "JOE CLARK STYLE"

In the late 1990s, my dual worlds of education and music intersected in a way that continues to resonate deeply with me. By day, I was a middle school social studies teacher in the Detroit Public Schools, striving to inspire young minds. By night, I was managing Proof's hip hop group, 5 ELA (5 Elementz), and later served as Vice President of his label, Iron Fist Records. Proof, the lyrical mastermind of D12, was not only a gifted artist but also a profoundly thoughtful human being whose impact stretched far beyond the music.

Photo of the 1st Motor City Hip Hop Revue at Shooter's in Big Rapids, MI with 5 ELA (Mudd, Thyme, Proof), Keeli Lackey, myself and Poe Whosaine and his group members. (Photo credit: Craig Huckaby)

Our conversations often revolved around the power of hip hop culture and its impact on youth. As a teacher, I was very aware of how certain lyrics influenced young minds, and I didn't shy away from expressing my concerns. Proof, despite his larger-than-life persona, listened even when I didn't think he was. Being ever observant, he found ways to bridge the gap between his artistry and my mission as an educator. Proof didn't just hear me; he acted.

Proof and I on The Heidelberg Project at rally for the 10th anniversary of the Million Man March. (Photo Credit: Kahn Davison)

Iron Fist Records staff (220 Bagley St. Detroit, MI)

One moment that still humbles me was when Proof, fresh off a red-eye flight from Los Angeles after attending a music awards show (maybe the MTV Music Awards with Eminem), made it a point to come straight from the airport to my first-period 7th-grade social studies class. There, in pure Proof style, with a big smile on his face he waited UNDER MY DESK for me to take attendance and then jumped out! To the utter surprise of my students who had just saw him the night before on TV there he was to greet them in person with his infectious energy! That gesture wasn't for show — it was Proof's way of giving back, recognizing the cultural currency that comes with being a celebrity, and, more importantly, emphasizing the value of staying accessible to the community.

Proof got a kick out of hearing the students call me Mr. Bell so he took a jab. He's words "Life is funny but it's necessary." and "Paths cross not for reasons but for purpose." have come to mean so much over the years. But perhaps the most soul touching gift he gave me was a handwritten poem titled "Joe Clark Style." At first glance, it seemed like a nod to the iconic 1989 film *Lean on Me* and its unforgettable scene where Joe Clark, played by Morgan Freeman, confronts a struggling student with the blunt question: "You smoke crack, don't you?" It was a moment of tough love meant to jolt the student into recognizing the consequences of destructive behavior. Proof's acrostic poem used the line "You Smoke Crack Don't You" as its framework, each letter beginning a new line that weaved together reflections on addiction, societal struggles, and personal redemption. At the time, I didn't fully grasp the depth of the poem. I was moved by the gesture but set it aside as life continued at its usual fast pace. It wasn't until after Proof's tragic and untimely death that I revisited the poem and its deeper meaning emerged.

Proof's "Joe Clark Style" was more than a nod to a pop culture film; like Proof himself, it was deeply layered and nuanced, with wisdom, humor, and self-reflection. Lines like "Oppressing my consciousness" and "Know your root to identify your future" spoke directly to the struggles many of my students faced daily — struggles that Proof himself intimately

14

understood. Through the poem, he mirrored the film's themes of tough love and transformation, infusing them with his own spiritual and existential reflections: "Christ knew himself to know God" and "Understanding you are all, ends all problems."

But there was also humor tucked into its structure — a wit that only Proof could deliver. It took me months to realize that embedded within the poem's lines was a playful jab, as if he were saying, "Don't take yourself too seriously, Khalid."

Reflecting on that poem now, I see it as a testament to Proof's genius. He wasn't just a rapper or an entertainer; he was a philosopher, a storyteller, and a bridge between worlds. His gift to me wasn't just a poem — it was a reminder of the transformative power of words and the importance of using them responsibly.

> **Joe Clark Style**
> Yearning for the next hi
> Oppressing my consciousness
> Unusual for the self knowing to
> Suffer the plite of the karnal
> Mind, finding themselves placed and
> Observed in the matrix
> Choadic ways of living are
> Expected to the disorderly
> Causaulities are usually applauded
> Released back to the most high
> Accurately according to wisdom
> Christ knew himself to know God
> Know your root to Identify your future in the
> Droppin seeds or fruits
> Open ya' mind to see
> Nimrod in the pipe, blunt, or needle
> torturing yourself to escape strain and stress of
> Yesterday, defaults your program of your hologram
> Over the master there is but nothing
> Understanding your are all, ends all problems
> now go head jump.

In the years since Proof's passing (it's been 18 years), I've often thought about what he meant to the hip hop community and to me personally. His ability to listen, to create, and to inspire was unparalleled. His presence in my classroom that day wasn't just for my students; it was for me too — a reminder that the work we do, whether in the studio or the classroom, has the potential to shape lives.

Proof's legacy lives on, not just in his music but in the countless lives he touched with his generosity, brilliance, and humor. And for me, his "Joe Clark Style" remains a cherished artifact in the archive of the Black History 101 Mobile Museum — a piece of poetry that continues to teach, challenge, and inspire, just like the man who wrote it.

PROFESSOR GRIFF AND THE BLACK HISTORY 101 MOBILE MUSEUM: A JOURNEY OF COLLABORATION

I can't tell the story of the Black History 101 Mobile Museum without talking about how deeply Public Enemy shaped my path. As a young man, albums like *It Takes a Nation of Millions to Hold Us Back* and *Fear of a Black Planet* were more than music—they were an education. Chuck D, Professor Griff, and the rest of the group opened my eyes to histories and truths that the schools I attended never even touched. Their lyrics challenged me to think critically, to question the world around me, and to embrace the power of Black culture. In hip hop music, Public Enemy was my first introduction to the idea that history isn't just in textbooks; it's in the stories, struggles, and triumphs of our people.

In 2003, when I first met Professor Griff after one of his lectures in Detroit, it felt like everything had come full circle. I had admired his work for years, and now here I was, introducing myself as someone who had been inspired by his message to create something of my own. After his lecture, I approached him, shared my vision for the Black History 101 Mobile Museum, and we exchanged numbers. I'll never forget how quickly he responded: "Give me a call whenever you're ready for me to get involved." That moment solidified for me that this wasn't just a chance encounter—it was the beginning of a meaningful collaboration.

Initially, I asked him to contribute to a couple of projects at Iron Fist Records. He submitted a track called Rootz Are the Proof for a project called Take the Land. Entrepreneur Robert Shumake and I were Executive Producers of the project. The day the national promotion of the project was release was the same day Proof was murdered. Needless to say the project never saw the light was day. In 2007, I took Griff up on his offer with the museum and invited him to be the guest speaker at the museum's first major campus event at the University of Michigan in Ann Arbor. This event was pivotal for the museum, a chance to introduce our work to a larger audience. Griff's presence elevated it to another level. His passion, insight, and ability to connect with the audience left a lasting impression. It was clear that his involvement brought something extraordinary to the museum's mission.

From that point forward, Griff became an integral part of the Black History 101 Mobile Museum, touring with me across the country. What I've learned from him during these years has been invaluable. His discipline and professionalism, honed during his years as Public Enemy's tour manager, pushed me to step up my game. Griff didn't just show up—he brought the same level of precision and dedication to our tours that he had mastered during his time with one of the greatest hip-hop groups in history. His approach to logistics, audience engagement, and the overall execution of events was a masterclass in how to run a successful operation.

Everywhere we went, Griff's ability to connect the artifacts in the museum to larger historical narratives and contemporary struggles left audiences in awe. He doesn't just speak—he educates, inspires, and challenges people to think deeply and critically about their history and their role in shaping the future.

As we celebrate the 30th anniversary of the Black History 101 Mobile Museum, I am profoundly grateful for Griff's contributions. His involvement has been a collaboration rooted in shared values and a commitment to preserving and sharing the richness of Black history and culture. What started as a simple exchange of numbers in Detroit has grown into a powerful journey that continues to resonate with audiences across the country. Professor Griff's presence has been a gift, and with his input we have inspired audiences around the country and will continue to for years to come.

Paradise Gray, The Last Poets, Duminie Deporres, Professor Griff and others in Pittsburgh, PA

The Black History 101 Mobile Museum's debut at the Lincoln Center in NY.

Awesome Dre, Quadir Lateef, Professor Griff and I at 5 E Gallery in Detroit.

Collector and exhibitor of Black history, Bill Costen, Griff, and I at the University of Massachusetts in Amherst.

Protecters of The Culture: Paradise, Griff, Duminie, and I.

Attending a tribute on the life and legacy of Muhammad Ali at Mosque Maryam in Chicago.

18

PROFESSOR GRIFF

CULTURAL CONFLICT AND THE CRISIS IN CONSCIOUSNESS

Wednesday September 19, 2018
Thursday September 20, 2018
7:00pm

$20 in Advance
$15 Student w/ID

Bro. Khalid el-Hakim
Black History Mobile Museum

Black History 101 Mobile Museum
$5.00 Entrance
Exhibit Doors Open at 3:00pm (Each Day)

TENNESSEE STATE UNIVERSITY
Elliott Hall
3500 John Merritt Blvd Nashville, TN 37209
DOORS OPEN @6PM LECTURE STARTS @7PM

Chapter 1

GROUNDBREAKERS & GAME-CHANGERS: REDEFINING EXCELLENCE

The Groundbreakers & Game-Changers: Redefining Excellence section celebrates the icons who defied expectations, shattered barriers, and redefined what it means to excel in their fields. From the arts to advocacy, these pioneers blazed trails that continue to inspire generations. The artifacts in this section of the Black History 101 Mobile Museum are a testament to the power of Black brilliance and resilience, capturing the stories of individuals who changed the narrative of history through their creativity, intellect, and determination.

Each artifact in this section tells a profound story of transformation. The Millie and Christine McCoy Cabinet Card (1851) reminds us how two women, born into the horrors of slavery, used their unique circumstances to overcome exploitation and become celebrated performers and philanthropists. The Frederick Douglass Spoon (Early 20th Century) and Frederick Douglass on Harper's Weekly Cover (1883) honor one of history's greatest abolitionists, whose voice continues to resonate as a beacon of freedom and equality.

In the realm of culture, we see the profound impact of artists like Jean-Michel Basquiat, whose New York Times Magazine Cover (1985) and Beat Bop Album (1983) showcase his ability to fuse graffiti and high art, bringing hip-hop into the global fine art conversation. Similarly, Madam C.J. Walker's Tan-Off Product Advertisement highlights her groundbreaking achievements as America's first self-made Black female millionaire, demonstrating entrepreneurial brilliance that uplifted Black women nationwide.

The enduring influence of Black creativity is further celebrated through items like Langston Hughes' Handwritten Letter (1960) and the Amiri Baraka Cover of Negro Digest (1969), both of which reflect the literary excellence and activism of the Harlem Renaissance and the Black Arts Movement. Savion Glover's "Footnotes" Program captures the rhythmic genius of a tap dance icon, while Serena Williams' Business of Fashion Magazine Cover (2019) highlights how she has transcended sports to become a cultural and business powerhouse.

These artifacts are not just historical relics—they are living testimonies to the extraordinary achievements of Black people who challenged the status quo and redefined what was possible. They serve as a source of inspiration, proving that the fight for excellence and representation is timeless and deeply rooted in the broader struggle for justice and equality.

MILLIE AND CHRISTINE MCCOY CABINET CARD: TWINS WHO SHARED THEIR GIFTS WITH THE WORLD.

This original cabinet card photograph features Millie and Christine McCoy, conjoined twins famously known as "The Two-Headed Nightingale." Born into slavery on July 11, 1851, in North Carolina, the twins were sold multiple times to men who exhibited them as "oddities" in road shows across America and England, including the Barnum circus. Despite their exploitation, their resilience and talent turned them into celebrated performers.

After the Emancipation Proclamation, their former owner traveled to Britain with their mother to reclaim them from a fraudulent exhibitor. Upon returning to the United States, the twins continued to perform widely, captivating audiences with their ability to sing, dance, play piano, and converse in five languages. Their fame extended internationally, and they even performed for Queen Victoria during a return visit to England.

The McCoys were billed under titles such as *"The Carolina Twins," "The Two-Headed Nightingale,"* and *"The Eighth Wonder of the World."* Despite the challenges they faced, Millie and Christine used their financial success to support Black schools and churches, leaving a lasting legacy of philanthropy and empowerment.

On October 8, 1912, Millie passed away from tuberculosis, and Christine followed just 12 hours later. Their lives, though marked by adversity, were a testament to resilience, talent, and generosity, and this photograph captures a moment in their extraordinary journey from enslavement to international fame and advocacy.

FREDERICK DOUGLASS SPOON (EARLY 20TH CENTURY)

A commemorative artifact honoring the abolitionist's legacy. This is a commemorative silver spoon featuring a profile portrait of Frederick Douglass, the famed abolitionist, orator, and writer. The bowl of the spoon bears an intricately engraved image of Douglass along with the words "Frederick Douglass" and "Born in Maryland." The handle is adorned with a decorative chain-link design, symbolizing the breaking of the chains of slavery and Douglass's pivotal role in the abolitionist movement.

Each link of the chain is inscribed with key dates or milestones, likely significant to Douglass's life or the broader history of emancipation and civil rights. The craftsmanship of the spoon demonstrates its creation as a tribute to Douglass's legacy and his enduring influence on the fight for freedom and equality.

As both a functional object and a historical artifact, this spoon serves as a unique representation of how Douglass's image and message were preserved and celebrated in American culture. It highlights the intersection of everyday utility and commemorative art, connecting the legacy of Douglass to the daily lives of those inspired by his remarkable contributions.

Frederick Douglass on Harper's Weekly Cover (1883): Recognizing Douglass's influence on American society.

On November 24, 1883, Frederick Douglass was profiled on the cover of *Harper's Weekly*, a prominent 19th-century American publication known as "A Journal of Civilization." The issue features a striking engraving of Frederick Douglass, one of the most influential abolitionists, orators, and statesmen in American history. The detailed portrait captures Douglass in his later years, with his iconic white hair, exuding dignity and wisdom.

The inclusion of Douglass on the cover reflects his status as a prominent figure in the fight for civil rights and racial equality during the Reconstruction era and beyond. At this time, Douglass was widely recognized as a leading voice against racism, a champion of suffrage for both African Americans and women, and a advocate for justice. The accompanying article inside the issue explores his life, work, and enduring impact on American society.

This cover is not only a testament to Douglass's legacy but also a historical artifact that illustrates how his contributions were acknowledged during his lifetime. It remains a powerful symbol of the ongoing struggle for equality and the transformative role of individuals like Douglass in shaping the course of American history.

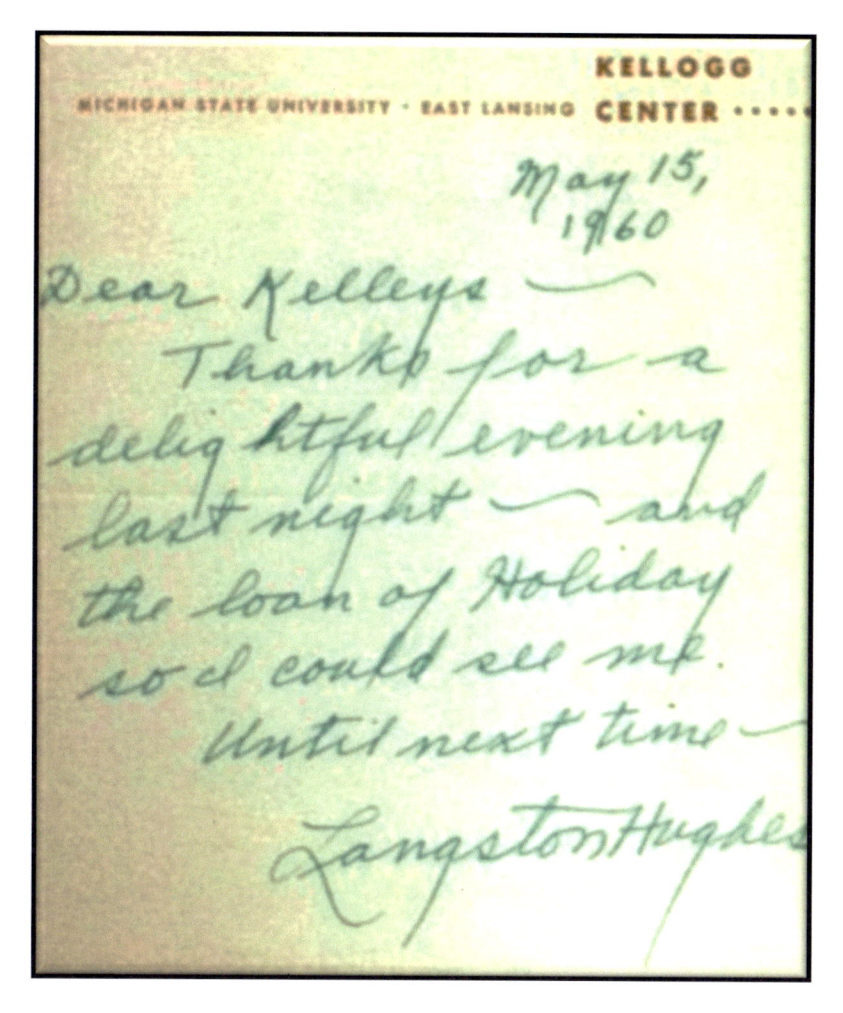

> May 15, 1960
>
> Dear Kelleys —
> Thanks for a delightful evening last night — and the loan of Holiday so I could see me.
> Until next time —
> Langston Hughes

LANGSTON HUGHES HANDWRITTEN LETTER (1960): A PERSONAL GLIMPSE INTO THE HARLEM RENAISSANCE ICON.

Penned in the beautiful handwriting of Langston Hughes on Michigan State University stationery, showcases his deep appreciation and humility. In the letter, Hughes thanks the Kelley's for their kind hospitality, expressing gratitude for the welcome extended to him during his travels. His handwriting is both elegant and deliberate, reflecting the thoughtful nature of his correspondence.

This artifact not only highlights Hughes's human connection but also offers a rare personal insight into his character beyond his monumental literary contributions. As one of the most celebrated figures of the Harlem Renaissance, Hughes's graciousness and genuine warmth are palpable through his words, serving as a reminder of his ability to bridge art and humanity in every aspect of his life. He was known to use green ink often in correspondence.

Ira Aldridge Sculpture: Honoring the first Black actor to perform Othello professionally.

This sculpture depicts Ira Aldridge in his acclaimed role as Othello, the Moor of Venice, from Shakespeare's iconic tragedy. Aldridge, an African American actor born in 1807, was one of the most prominent Shakespearean actors of the 19th century and the first Black man to portray Othello on the professional stage. This striking piece captures the solemnity and depth of Aldridge's performance, emphasizing the emotional intensity he brought to the character.

The sculpture portrays Aldridge in a hooded cloak, holding what appears to be a symbolic representation of the ill-fated handkerchief central to the play's plot. The black and white tones of the sculpture underscore the racial themes central to *Othello*, highlighting the discrimination Othello endures and the tragic consequences of envy and betrayal.

Aldridge's groundbreaking career paved the way for Black actors in classical theater, despite the racial barriers of his time. His portrayal of Othello challenged stereotypes and brought dignity and humanity to the character, earning him recognition across Europe. This sculpture serves as a tribute to his legacy, celebrating his artistry and the historical significance of his contributions to theater.

Pullman Porter Hat: A Symbol of Dignity and Perseverance

The Pullman Porter hat represents an iconic chapter in African American labor history. Worn by porters working aboard luxury sleeping cars on the Pullman Company trains, this hat was more than just a uniform piece—it was a badge of professionalism, service, and pride. From the late 19th century through the mid-20th century, Pullman Porters played a vital role in shaping the Black middle class and advancing civil rights.

Pullman Porters were often subjected to long hours, low pay, and discriminatory treatment, yet they maintained an air of dignity and excellence in their work. Despite the challenges, these men were leaders within their communities, using their wages and experiences to support their families and fund educational opportunities. The Brotherhood of Sleeping Car Porters, the first Black-led labor union to be recognized by a major corporation, emerged from their ranks in 1925 under the leadership of A. Philip Randolph, marking a significant step toward labor equality.

As Randolph once said, *"We want the full recognition of our manhood, our citizenship, and our dignity, not only as laborers but as human beings."* This quote encapsulates the spirit of the Pullman Porters, whose work and fight for equality extended beyond the rails to uplift their communities and demand respect in a society that often sought to deny them their rightful place.

This hat serves as a testament to the resilience and determination of the Pullman Porters, whose contributions laid the foundation for both economic progress and the broader struggle for racial justice in the United States.

MADAM C.J. WALKER'S TAN-OFF PRODUCT HIGHLIGHTING WALKER'S IMPACT AS AMERICA'S FIRST SELF-MADE BLACK FEMALE MILLIONAIRE.

Madam C.J. Walker (1867–1919) was one of the first self-made female millionaires in America and a trailblazer for Black entrepreneurship. Born Sarah Breedlove to formerly enslaved parents, she rose from poverty through hard work, ingenuity, and a commitment to uplifting her community. Walker developed a successful line of haircare products tailored to the needs of Black women, revolutionizing the beauty industry by addressing a demographic that had long been overlooked.

Beyond her business achievements, Walker was a philanthropist and activist, advocating for racial and gender equity. She used her wealth to support organizations like the NAACP and donated generously to educational institutions and civil rights causes. Her company not only provided beauty products but also created employment opportunities for thousands of Black women as sales agents, enabling them to achieve financial independence and social mobility.

While some of her products, like *Tan-Off,* reflect the complexities of navigating the oppressive beauty standards of her time, Madam C.J. Walker's legacy endures as a symbol of empowerment, resilience, and innovation.

Madam C.J. Walker College of Beauty Culture Advertisement

This advertisement promotes the Madam C.J. Walker College of Beauty Culture, a network of training schools for aspiring beauty professionals. The ad invites individuals to enroll in low-cost, pay-as-you-go courses across major cities like Chicago, Dallas, Indianapolis, Kansas City, and Washington, D.C., offering both day and night classes for full-time or part-time learners. The tagline encourages a "glamorous, profitable career as a professional beautician," emphasizing empowerment through education and financial independence.

The ad highlights the success of the "Madam Walker way" of beauty training, which taught students to use Walker's renowned products, such as her Double-Strength Scalp Ointment, Hair & Scalp Preparation, and Glossine. These products, known for their efficacy in addressing common hair care issues, also played a key role in students' education, ensuring graduates provided results that kept customers returning.

A map visually illustrates the geographic reach of Walker's institutions, showcasing their accessibility across the United States. Additionally, testimonials and images of school principals lend a personal touch to the campaign, reinforcing the message of opportunity and prestige.

This ad is not just a call to action but a testament to Madam C.J. Walker's enduring legacy. By offering Black women the chance to achieve professional success and economic independence, the Walker College of Beauty Culture became a cornerstone of empowerment during an era of limited opportunities for African Americans.

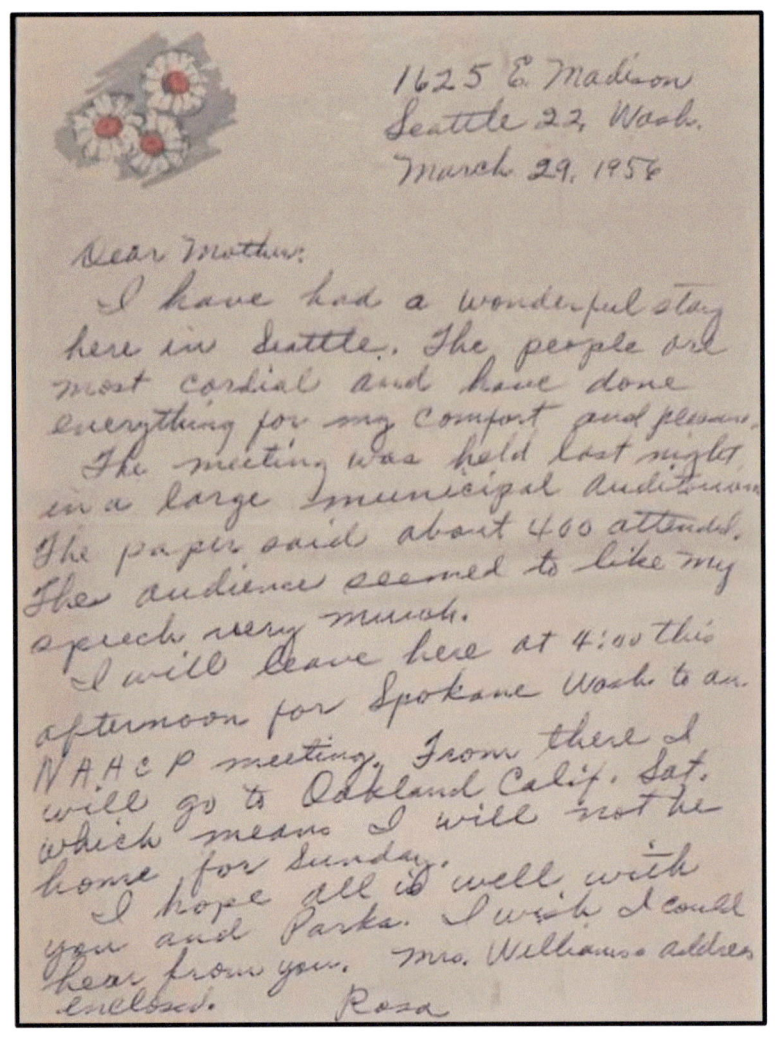

Letter from Rosa Parks to Her Mother (March 29, 1956): A Glimpse Into Her Civil Rights Journey

Rosa Parks wrote this letter to her mother on March 29, 1956 during a stop in Seattle, Washington, while Parks was traveling to raise awareness and support for the burgeoning Civil Rights Movement. In the letter, Parks describes her reception in Seattle, where she spoke at a meeting attended by about 400 people at a municipal auditorium. She notes the warm hospitality she received and the positive response to her speech, reflecting her role as a key figure in mobilizing communities across the nation.

The letter is deeply rooted in the context of the Montgomery Bus Boycott, which began on December 5, 1955, after Rosa Parks' historic arrest for refusing to give up her seat on a segregated bus. By March 1956, the boycott had entered its fourth month, becoming a critical moment in the fight against racial segregation. Parks' travels, as referenced in the letter, were part of her efforts to connect with civil rights organizations such as the NAACP, gather support, and sustain the momentum of the boycott.

The letter offers a rare and intimate glimpse into Parks' dedication, resilience, and the immense pressure she faced as a symbol of resistance. It also highlights the broader network of activists and supporters working tirelessly to dismantle segregation. The letter serves as both a historical artifact and a reminder of the sacrifices made by Parks and countless others in the struggle for equality and justice.

Dr. Percy L. Julian Cover on *The Oracle* (1950): Highlights his contributions to science and racial equity.

Dr. Percy Julian is featured on this March 1950 issue of *The Oracle*, the official magazine of the Omega Psi Phi Fraternity honoring him as "Man of the Year." Dr. Julian, a distinguished member of Omega Psi Phi, is depicted in a laboratory setting surrounded by scientific equipment, emphasizing his groundbreaking contributions to science and innovation.

Dr. Julian, an acclaimed African American chemist and Omega man, is celebrated for his pioneering work in synthesizing medicinal compounds such as cortisone, steroids, and hormones, which revolutionized the pharmaceutical industry. Despite facing significant racial discrimination throughout his career, he persevered to become one of the most celebrated chemists of his time, earning numerous accolades and breaking barriers for African Americans in STEM field

This cover not only highlights Dr. Julian's dedication to science but also reflects the values of Omega Psi Phi in uplifting excellence and promoting education and leadership. His inclusion in *The Oracle* serves as a testament to his remarkable achievements, his alignment with the fraternity's mission, and the profound impact of his work on medicine, society, and the advancement of African Americans.

**AUTOGRAPHED PHOTO OF
AIMÉ CÉSAIRE: A TRIBUTE TO THE CO-FOUNDER OF THE NÉGRITUDE
MOVEMENT.**

      This autographed photograph of Aimé Césaire, the influential poet, playwright, and politician from Martinique, holds deep personal and historical meaning for me. Inscribed with the message "À Khalid el Hakim, amical salut" ("To Khalid el-Hakim, friendly greetings"), it represents a symbolic connection between two individuals dedicated to preserving the cultural and historical legacy of the African diaspora.

      As a co-founder of the Négritude movement, Césaire was a powerful voice for affirming Black identity in the face of colonial oppression. His literary works, including *Notebook of a Return to My Native Land,* and his political career were instrumental in shaping global discussions on racial identity, anti-colonialism, and cultural pride.

      This photograph also tells the story of a missed but meaningful connection. Césaire became aware of the Black History 101 Mobile Museum through a mutual acquaintance in Martinique. Acknowledging the museum's vital work, he extended an invitation for me to share the collection with him in Martinique. Although we never met due to his passing in 2008, this signed photograph was sent as a gesture of admiration and support for the museum's mission.
40

JEAN-MICHEL BASQUIAT NEW YORK TIMES MAGAZINE COVER (1985): SHOWCASING HIS RISE AS A GRAFFITI-INSPIRED ART PHENOMENON.

The New York Times Magazine featured the renowned artist Jean-Michel Basquiat on February 10, 1985. The headline, *"New Art, New Money: The Marketing of an American Artist,"* captures the rise of Basquiat as a cultural phenomenon in the art world during the 1980s. The cover image portrays Basquiat seated barefoot, exuding an air of confidence and contemplation, surrounded by his distinctive, graffiti-inspired artwork. His suit contrasts with the raw, vibrant art behind him, symbolizing his navigation of both the elite art market and his urban, street-art roots.

This cover highlights Basquiat's meteoric rise to fame as a self-taught artist who transitioned from graffiti on New York City walls to being one of the most celebrated and financially successful contemporary artists of his time. His work, a fusion of abstract, street-art aesthetics with commentary on race, identity, and power, resonated deeply with the cultural zeitgeist. The article explores not only his artistic genius but also the commodification of his art, raising questions about the intersection of creativity and capitalism.

Basquiat's presence on the cover of a major publication like The New York Times Magazine symbolizes his lasting impact on the art world and his role in breaking barriers as a young Black artist in a predominantly white industry.

JEAN-MICHEL BASQUIAT'S BEAT BOP ALBUM (1983): FUSING HIP-HOP AND AVANT-GARDE ART.

"Beat Bop," one of the rarest album of hip hop culture, features the iconic artwork of Jean-Michel Basquiat, a reflection of his dynamic visual style and his contribution to the hip-hop and downtown New York art scenes. Released in 1983 on Tartown Record Co., this album is a collaboration between hip-hop pioneers Rammellzee and K-Rob, with Basquiat serving as producer. Only 500 copies of the original pressing were made, making it a highly sought-after collector's item in both music and art circles.

The cover, designed entirely by Basquiat, showcases his signature aesthetic—chaotic scribbles, symbols, crowns, and cryptic text—offering a visceral glimpse into his artistic psyche. The imagery complements the experimental and avant-garde nature of the music within, which blends surreal storytelling, atmospheric beats, and unconventional rap flows.

"Beat Bop" holds a unique place in history, as it bridges the worlds of fine art, hip-hop culture, and underground music. Often referred to as a precursor to modern alternative hip-hop, this album is a cultural artifact of the early 1980s, a time when Basquiat and his contemporaries were reshaping the boundaries of art and music. Its rarity, coupled with its historical and artistic significance, cements its status as one of the most coveted vinyl records of all time.

SERENA WILLIAMS BUSINESS OF FASHION MAGAZINE COVER (2019): SHOWCASING HER DOMINANCE IN SPORTS AND FASHION.

Tennis great Serena Williams is featured on the cover of this special edition issue of *The Business of Fashion* (BOF), dated April 2019. The theme, "Modern Entrepreneurs," highlights Serena not only as a world-renowned tennis champion but also as a powerful businesswoman and fashion entrepreneur. Known for breaking barriers both on and off the court, Serena embodies empowerment, innovation, and excellence, which aligns with the issue's focus on trailblazers in entrepreneurship and design.

The cover showcases Serena in a poised and confident pose, wearing a sleek blue outfit that reflects her fashion-forward persona.

I met Serena in LA at a mall and she personally signed it for me. Her autograph emphasizes her connection with her fans and supporters, making this magazine a prized keepsake that celebrates her multifaceted legacy as an athlete, entrepreneur, and cultural icon.

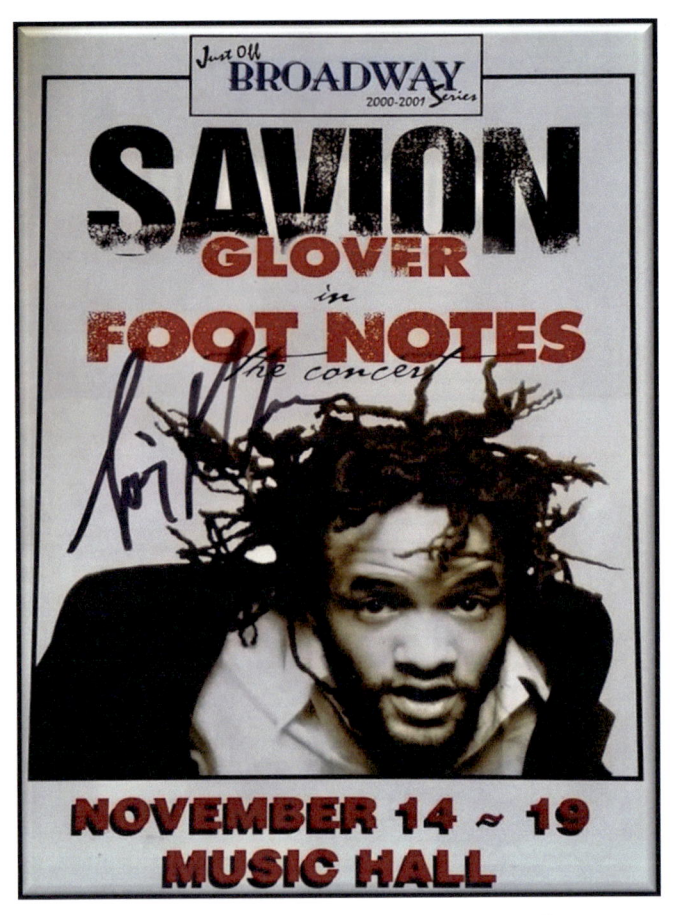

SAVION GLOVER "FOOTNOTES" PROGRAM: CELEBRATING THE ARTISTRY OF THE LEGENDARY TAP DANCER.

  This is a signed playbill from Savion Glover's *Foot Notes: The Concert*, part of the 2000-2001 "Just Off Broadway Series." The performance ran from November 14 to November 19 at the Music Hall and featured Glover, a trailblazing tap dancer and choreographer, renowned for his innovative contributions to the art of tap dance.

  FootNotes was a celebration of rhythm, sound, and movement, showcasing Glover's mastery of tap dance as a form of percussive storytelling. Widely celebrated for his work on Broadway in *Bring in 'da Noise, Bring in 'da Funk* and in films like *Happy Feet*, Glover has been a cultural icon who bridges the worlds of tradition and modernity in dance.

  I had the privilege of witnessing this historic performance and asked Savion to sign the program. This autographed playbill stands as a cherished keepsake, capturing the essence of Glover's groundbreaking artistry. It reflects not only his dedication to preserving the rich legacy of tap but also his innovative spirit in redefining the art form and pushing its boundaries into exciting new realms.

JIMI HENDRIX ON THE COVER OF ROLLING STONE (1970): RECOGNIZING HIS REVOLUTIONARY INFLUENCE ON ROCK MUSIC.

Rolling Stone paid tribute the legendary guitarist Jimi Hendrix on October 15 1970, featuring a striking black-and-white portrait of the artist. The image captures Hendrix's intense gaze and signature style, including his untamed hair and military-inspired jacket, which became a hallmark of his persona. The text below the photo, "Jimi Hendrix 1945-1970," honors his life and legacy, emphasizing the profound impact he had on music during his brief but revolutionary career.

This cover was published shortly after Hendrix's untimely death on September 18, 1970, at the age of 27. Rolling Stone, a premier voice in music journalism, recognized Hendrix's unparalleled contributions to rock and roll, celebrating him as a visionary who transformed the electric guitar into a powerful instrument of artistic expression.

Jimi Hendrix's influence extended far beyond music; he became a cultural icon of the 1960s, embodying the era's spirit of experimentation, freedom, and rebellion. His innovative techniques, such as feedback and distortion, redefined the possibilities of sound, earning him a permanent place in the pantheon of musical greats. This cover stands as a timeless homage to a trailblazer whose artistry continues to inspire generations.

Amiri Baraka Cover of Negro Digest (1969): Reflecting his blend of activism and literature.

In January 1969, Amiri Baraka, then known as Leroi Jones, was featured on the cover of *Negro Digest*, during a pivotal moment in his career and the broader Black Arts Movement. The issue highlights Baraka's transformation as a cultural and political revolutionary, exploring his embrace of Black nationalism, Islam, and the power of art to enact social change.

Through an in-depth interview, Baraka delves into themes of identity, resistance, and the role of Black literature and theater in confronting systemic racism. His piercing gaze on the cover symbolizes his unapologetic stance as a leader in the cultural revolution of the 1960s, where art, politics, and activism intertwined to create new possibilities for Black liberation.

This artifact stands as a testament to Baraka's enduring impact on literature, performance, and the fight for cultural autonomy, capturing a moment when the pen and the voice were equally powerful weapons in the struggle for freedom and justice.

THE BRONZE VENUS MOVIE POSTER FEATURING LENA HORNE (1943): CELEBRATING ONE OF HOLLYWOOD'S FIRST BLACK SUPERSTARS.

Lena Horne is prominently featured on the movie poster for the musical, The Bronze Venus. As one of Hollywood's first Black superstars, Horne shines in this role, blending her unparalleled beauty, elegance, and vocal talent. The poster captures her radiant presence, showcasing her as a symbol of grace and sophistication during an era when opportunities for Black performers in mainstream cinema were severely limited.

The film, originally titled *The Duke is Tops*, was re-released as *The Bronze Venus* to capitalize on Horne's rising fame, emphasizing her status as a trailblazer for African Americans in entertainment. The vibrant artwork of the poster reflects the glamour of the 1940s while honoring Horne's groundbreaking achievements in breaking racial barriers in Hollywood.

This artifact represents not only Lena Horne's remarkable career but also a significant cultural moment when Black excellence began to challenge and redefine industry norms, paving the way for future generations of performers.

Battle of the Stars Flyer (1960s): A snapshot of Motown's golden era, featuring The Temptations and Mary Wells.

This vintage flyer advertises a "Big Show and Dance" titled the "Battle of the Stars", held on Saturday, March 7, at the historic Graystone Ballroom. The event, running from 9 p.m. to 2 a.m., features a showdown between two legendary Motown groups: The Contours, best known for their hit *"Do You Love Me,"* and The Temptations, performing their classic *"The Way You Do the Things You Do."*

Adding to the star-studded lineup is a special appearance by Mary Wells, the "First Lady of Motown," known for her soulful hit *"What's Easy for Two Is So Hard for One."* The Choker Campbell Band, a celebrated Motown ensemble, provided the live music accompaniment, ensuring a high-energy and unforgettable night of dancing and entertainment.

The flyer reflects the energy of the 1960s Motown music scene, with its playful hand-drawn elements, bold fonts, and musical notes, capturing the excitement surrounding these iconic performers. Tickets for the event were priced at just $1.50 in advance or $2.00 at the door, a bargain for witnessing some of the greatest names in music history.

This flyer is a nostalgic artifact from a time when the Graystone Ballroom was a hub for Motown's rising stars, showcasing the incredible talent that shaped the sound of Detroit and defined a generation of music lovers.

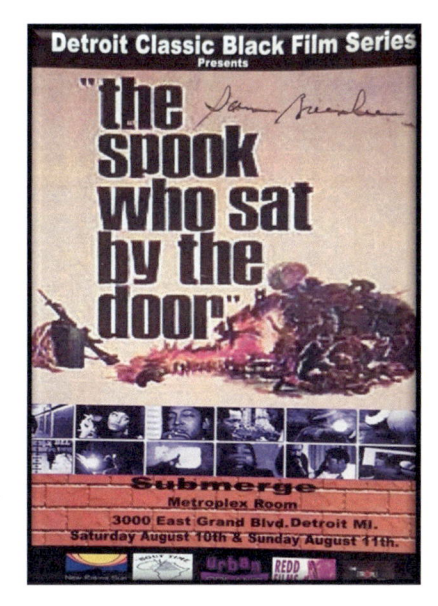

LOBBY CARD AND FLYER FOR *THE SPOOK WHO SAT BY THE DOOR*: THE STORY OF THE FIRST CIA AGENT.

    This lobby card promotes the 1973 film *The Spook Who Sat by the Door*, directed by Ivan Dixon and based on Sam Greenlee's provocative novel of the same name. The card features a still from the film, depicting two men playing pool in a dimly lit urban setting. The gritty ambiance mirrors the film's raw exploration of racial dynamics and revolutionary resistance. Central to the scene is Dan Freeman, portrayed by Lawrence Cook, standing by the pool table in a denim jacket, holding a cue. His calm and composed demeanor contrasts sharply with the film's intense and politically charged narrative.

    The bold yellow text highlights the film's title, emphasizing its provocative double meaning. It serves as both a racial slur and a nod to Freeman's role as a token Black CIA operative who later uses his covert training to organize a Black revolutionary movement. Upon its release, the film was highly controversial, offering a scathing critique of systemic racism, tokenism, and the fight for Black liberation in America. This lobby card encapsulates the film's blend of everyday realism and revolutionary aspirations, making it a significant artifact from the Blaxploitation era with an uncommon focus on political resistance.

    The flyer is from an event I sponsored in Detroit in 2007, where Sam Greenlee screened the film. This event, co-sponsored with Drake Phifer of Urban Organic, Katrina Redd of Redd Films, Pharoah Muhammad of 'Bout Time Publishing, and Madd Mike Banks of the legendary techno group Underground Resistance, drew packed audiences for two screenings. Sam Greenlee signed this flyer for me, making it a treasured keepsake from an unforgettable evening celebrating his groundbreaking work.

DR. JOHN HENRIK CLARKE SIGNED PRESS PHOTO: HONORING THE HISTORIAN AND PAN-AFRICANIST.

Dr. John Henrik Clarke, an influential scholar, historian, and activist who played a significant role in the development of Africana studies. Dr. Clarke is captured here in a formal pose, exuding the dignity and intellectual rigor for which he was known. The autograph includes a personalized message, reflecting his engagement with those who admired his work. This rare, signed photograph is a testament to his enduring legacy as a thought leader and advocate for African and African American history.

Chapter 2

RISE UP: ARTIFACTS OF RESISTANCE & LIBERATION

The artifacts in this section illuminate the powerful stories of individuals, movements, and moments that have shaped the ongoing struggle for justice and equity. From the Civil Rights Movement to the Black Power era, and from global calls for peace to the unity of cultural gatherings, these artifacts reflect the courage and determination of those who stood up against systemic oppression. They are not just relics of the past; they are vibrant reminders of the resilience and ingenuity that fuel the fight for justice.

Each item documented here represents a piece of history—a thread in the broader tapestry of resistance. The World War I poster, "The Colored Man Is No Slacker," challenges the pervasive racist narratives of the time by honoring the bravery of African American soldiers. Malcolm X's flyers and photographs embody his call for self-reliance and critical engagement with systemic oppression, as he proclaimed, "You can't separate peace from freedom because no one can be at peace unless he has his freedom." Similarly, Dr. Martin Luther King Jr.'s speech, preserved in the album *Why I Oppose the War in Vietnam*, connects the fight for civil rights with global struggles for justice, declaring, "Injustice anywhere is a threat to justice everywhere."

The collection also includes items that symbolize grassroots organizing and the solidarity of everyday people. The March on Washington pennant, emblazoned with "I Was There," captures the pride and unity of the 250,000 individuals who gathered to demand civil and economic rights. The Million Man March bumper sticker similarly represents the power of mass mobilization, as Minister Louis Farrakhan urged Black men to embrace atonement and responsibility, saying, "Atonement means to make amends, to repair a wrong, and to bring peace to a troubled soul."

Together, these artifacts remind us that the struggle for liberation is as much about individual courage as it is about collective action. They offer a glimpse into the sacrifices and triumphs of those who paved the way for progress, forcing us to confront uncomfortable truths while inspiring us to continue their work. As Malcolm X once stated, "The future belongs to those who prepare for it today." These artifacts are a testament to that preparation—tools of resistance and liberation that echo across generations, urging us to rise up and carry forward the legacy of justice and equity.

Iron Shackles: Symbols of Oppression and Resistance

These shackles are a grim reminder of the transatlantic slave trade and the brutal system of slavery in the Americas, likely dating from the 18th to 19th centuries. Made of heavy iron, these chains were designed to bind enslaved Africans, restricting their movement and serving as instruments of oppression. The shackles were often used during the Middle Passage—transporting enslaved Africans across the Atlantic—and on plantations to subdue enslaved people.

The design of the shackles, with a collar for the neck and cuffs for the wrists or ankles connected by chains, demonstrates the inhumanity of slavery, reducing individuals to property and controlling them through physical restraint. However, such objects also symbolize the incredible resilience and resistance of the enslaved. Enslaved Africans resisted not just by escaping their bonds but through acts of rebellion, preservation of their culture, and the forging of community bonds despite overwhelming odds.

In many documented instances, enslaved individuals found ways to break free from these shackles, both literally and metaphorically. Some used ingenuity to unlock or sever the chains, escaping captivity and forming Maroon communities or joining abolitionist movements. The shackles, therefore, serve as a powerful symbol—not just of the cruelty endured but also of the unyielding spirit of those who resisted and fought for freedom. These artifacts remind us of the struggles and the strength of those who sought liberation under the harshest conditions imaginable.

A Cry for Freedom: 'Am I Not a Woman and a Sister' Coin

This 1838 coin features a powerful design inspired by the abolitionist movement, embodying the fight for the emancipation of enslaved women. The central image depicts a kneeling woman in chains, symbolizing the harsh reality of bondage. Encircling her are the poignant words, *"Am I Not a Woman & a Sister,"* a direct appeal to the humanity and morality of its audience.

This message was powerfully embodied by Sojourner Truth, a former enslaved woman who became a leading abolitionist and women's rights advocate. Her famous 1851 speech, *"Ain't I a Woman?"* delivered at the Ohio Women's Rights Convention, underscored the intersection of race and gender inequality. Truth's life and advocacy epitomized the struggles symbolized by this coin, as she dedicated her voice to fighting for freedom, equality, and dignity for African American women.

This coin served as both a symbol and tool of advocacy, circulating as a call to action during the abolitionist era. It stands as a reminder of the resilience and courage of women like Sojourner Truth, who fought tirelessly for justice and human rights.

"The Colored Man Is No Slacker" Poster (WWI Era): Recognizing Black Patriotism during WWI.

The *"The Colored Man Is No Slacker"* poster is a patriotic illustration from the World War I era that highlights the contributions of African Americans to the U.S. war effort. The artwork depicts an African American soldier in uniform tenderly holding the hands of a woman, possibly symbolizing his wife or loved one, as a regiment of Black soldiers marches in the background, carrying an American flag. The lush garden and peaceful surroundings suggest a sense of pride, dignity, and purpose in service to the nation.

The phrase *"The Colored Man Is No Slacker"* was a direct rebuttal to the racist stereotypes and narratives of the time that questioned the loyalty, bravery, and commitment of African Americans. During World War I, over 350,000 Black men served in the U.S. Army, many of them in segregated units, such as the famous Harlem Hellfighters (369th Infantry Regiment). Despite facing discrimination at home and in the military, these men demonstrated exceptional courage and patriotism, often earning respect on the battlefield that was denied to them in civilian life.

This poster was likely part of a broader campaign to encourage enlistment among African Americans and to counteract the widespread prejudice they faced. It also sought to bolster pride within the Black community, highlighting their integral role in defending the nation during a time of war.

Historically, posters like this one served as propaganda tools to both motivate and reshape public perception, yet they also reflected the harsh realities of the era: African American soldiers were often relegated to labor units and faced systemic discrimination despite their sacrifices. Nevertheless, the contributions of Black soldiers during World War I played a significant role in advancing the fight for civil rights, laying the groundwork for future movements for racial equality.

This poster remains a powerful artifact, celebrating the resilience, dignity, and patriotism of African Americans who served their country in the face of profound adversity.

NICHOLAS BIDDLE COMMEMORATIVE BADGE: A SYMBOL OF COURAGE AND SACRIFICE

This commemorative badge, created for the 1905 reunion of the First Defenders Association in Pottsville, Pennsylvania, honors Nicholas Biddle, a Black man recognized as the first to shed blood in the Civil War. The badge's inscription, "First man to shed blood in the rebellion, 1861-65," and its patriotic ribbon encapsulate the spirit of resistance and the sacrifices made by African Americans in the fight for freedom.

This badge exemplifies how individual acts of courage ignite broader movements for justice. Biddle's defiance of systemic racism by marching with Union troops—a revolutionary act in an era of deep racial oppression—aligns with the stories told by other artifacts in this collection. Like Malcolm X's proclamations of self-reliance and the Million Man March bumper sticker's call for accountability, this badge reminds us that liberation often begins with personal acts of bravery.

Biddle's bloodshed was not in vain; it was a symbolic spark in the Civil War, a conflict that would ultimately redefine the nation's values of freedom and equality. His legacy stands alongside artifacts like Dr. Martin Luther King Jr.'s speeches and March on Washington memorabilia, all of which reflect a history of resistance grounded in the pursuit of equity.

The badge is more than a relic of the past—it is a vibrant reminder that the fight for justice requires resilience and courage. Nicholas Biddle's story invites us to see liberation as an ongoing journey, urging us to rise up, confront systemic oppression, and carry forward the work of those who dared to defy injustice

MALCOLM X AND HIS BROTHERS PHOTOGRAPH (1963): A SNAPSHOT OF UNITY IN THE NATION OF ISLAM.

This rare 1963 photograph of Malcolm X (later El Hajj Malik Shabazz) with his brothers, Wilfred X and Philbert X (later Abdul Aziz Omar), captures a powerful moment of unity and shared commitment to the Nation of Islam's mission of Black empowerment and self-reliance. Malcolm, holding a flyer for an event featuring the Honorable Elijah Muhammad, reflects their dedication to advancing justice and equality during a pivotal period in the Civil Rights Movement.

The Little brothers' journey to activism was deeply influenced by their upbringing for a time in Lansing, Michigan, where their father, Earl Little, a Christian minister and follower of Marcus Garvey's teachings, instilled in them the importance of self-empowerment and racial pride. Tragically, their father was believed to have been killed by a white supremacist group due to his outspoken advocacy for Black self-determination. This traumatic experience, coupled with their father's Garveyite principles, laid the foundation for the brothers' eventual alignment with the teachings of the Honorable Elijah Muhammad and the Nation of Islam's philosophy of self-reliance.

This photograph carries personal significance for me, as it was donated by Wilfred Little, whom I knew as "Mr. Little," my neighbor on Snowden Street in Detroit. He was a beautiful human being who visited my class when I taught at the Detroit Job Corps and shared stories of his brother and the rest of his phenomenal family.

Malcolm X Speaking Engagement Flyer (1963): Promoting self-reliance and critical debates.

Malcolm X as a minister in the Nation of Islam is advertised for a lecture based on the teachings of The Honorable Elijah Muhammad. The event was set to take place on Sunday, October 1st, at 7:00 p.m. at the Garden of Prayer Baptist Church, 5326 So. Central Ave.

The flyer poses thought-provoking questions about the most pressing social and racial issues of the time, such as:
- "Integration, Segregation, or Separation?"
- "Which one has the most to offer Negro America?"
- "Which one has the most to offer White America?"
- "Is either choice the best solution for everybody, Black and White?"

The flyer claims that the only man in America with the answers is The Honorable Elijah Muhammad, the spiritual leader of the Nation of Islam. These answers were to be delivered by Malcolm X, referred to here as Elijah Muhammad's "New York Minister."

This artifact reflects the Nation of Islam's role in addressing the challenges faced by African Americans during the Civil Rights era. It underscores the Nation's focus on self-determination, racial pride, and the ideological debates surrounding integration versus separation. As a rising orator at the time, Malcolm X's participation in such events was instrumental in spreading the teachings of the The Honorable Elijah Muhammad and galvanizing audiences to consider alternative solutions to systemic racism and inequality.

FLYER OF ELIJAH MUHAMMAD SPEAKING AT COBO HALL DETROIT (1960s): REFLECTING THE NATION OF ISLAM'S EMPOWERMENT.

This flyer announces a major event featuring The Honorable Elijah Muhammad, leader of the Nation of Islam. The flyer promotes his personal appearance and speech, scheduled for June 11 at Cobo Arena in Detroit, Michigan, with doors opening at 12 noon.

The flyer's design is straightforward and powerful, with bold, capitalized text declaring "COMING TO DETROIT" and emphasizing the prominence of Elijah Muhammad's visit. His photograph, positioned to the right, shows him wearing his signature Nation of Islam hat adorned with a crescent and star, symbolizing his role as a spiritual leader.

This event reflects the growth of the Nation of Islam in Detroit, the city where the organization was founded in 1930. Elijah Muhammad's speeches were known for addressing issues of racial justice, Black empowerment, self-reliance, and the teachings of Islam as a solution to the systemic oppression faced by African Americans. Flyers like this played a key role in mobilizing supporters and spreading the message of the Nation of Islam across urban centers in America during the mid-20th century.

UNIVERSITY OF ISLAM PENNANT (1960S): SYMBOLIZING EDUCATION AND SELF-DETERMINATION.

This vintage pennant represents the University of Islam, the Nation of Islam's private educational institution. The deep purple felt banner features bold white lettering spelling "University of Islam," accompanied by the crescent moon and star symbol, an emblem of the Nation of Islam that signifies faith, unity, and enlightenment.

The schools were established to provide an alternative to public education, emphasizing self-reliance, discipline, and a curriculum rooted in Black empowerment and Islamic principles. These schools played a pivotal role in the Nation of Islam's mission to foster intellectual and moral development within the Black community, countering systemic racism and cultural erasure in mainstream education.

This pennant not only symbolizes pride in the institution but also serves as a testament to the Nation of Islam's broader efforts to create self-sufficient, community-focused infrastructures during the mid-20th century. It reflects the organization's commitment to nurturing a strong sense of identity and purpose among its students and members.

Muhammad Speaks: The weekly publication of the Nation of Islam.

This is the cover of an issue of *Muhammad Speaks*, the official newspaper of the Nation of Islam. The headline reads "The Nation of Islam History" and features prominent leaders and figures from the organization. At the center of the cover is the Honorable Elijah Muhammad, who led the Nation of Islam from 1934 until his passing in 1975. To his left is Master Fard Muhammad, the founder of the movement, credited with bringing the teachings of Islam to Black communities in the United States during the early 1930s.

Other notable figures include El-Hajj Malik El-Shabazz (Malcolm X), whose leadership as a minister under the Honorable Elijah Muhammad helped bring international recognition to the Nation of Islam. Also featured is Muhammad Ali, the legendary boxer who embraced the teachings of the Nation of Islam and became an outspoken advocate for civil rights. Imam Warith Deen Mohammed, the son of Elijah Muhammad, is also included; he played a pivotal role in transitioning the Nation of Islam into Al-Islam following his father's passing. Lastly, Minister Louis Farrakhan is prominently displayed; he revitalized the Nation of Islam in the late 1970s, continuing its mission of Black empowerment and self-reliance.

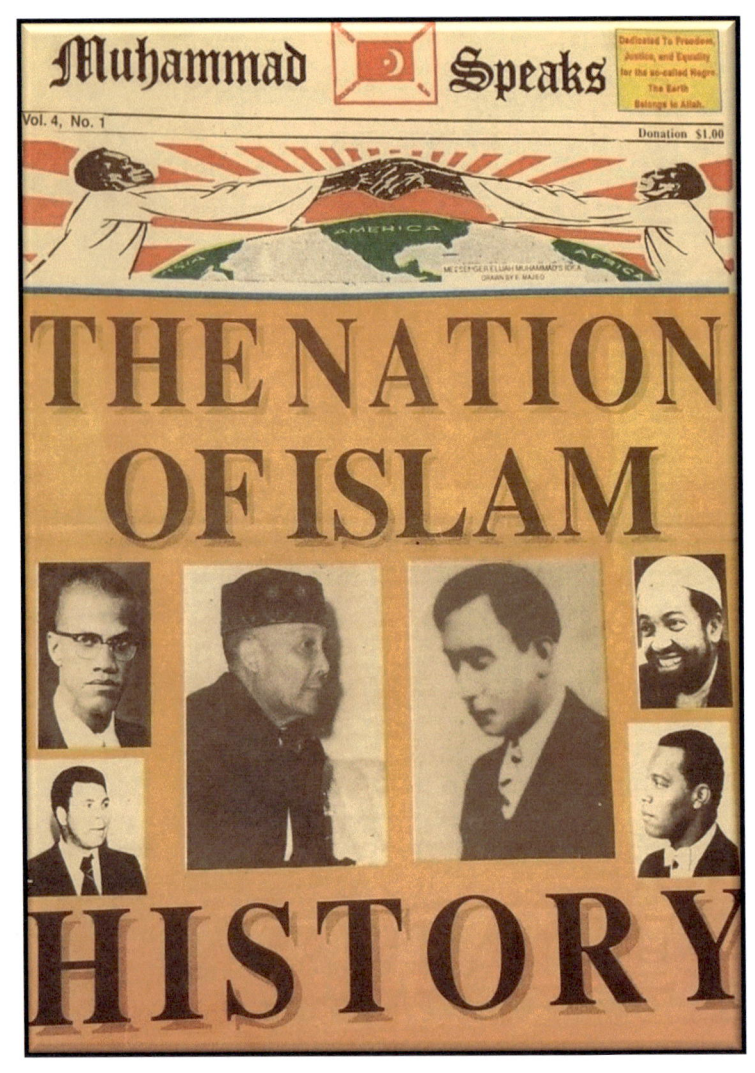

The imagery reflects the legacy of the Nation of Islam, including its contributions to Black liberation, self-determination, and spiritual upliftment. The cover symbolizes the collective impact of these individuals in shaping the history of the organization and their roles in the broader struggle for freedom, justice, and equality.

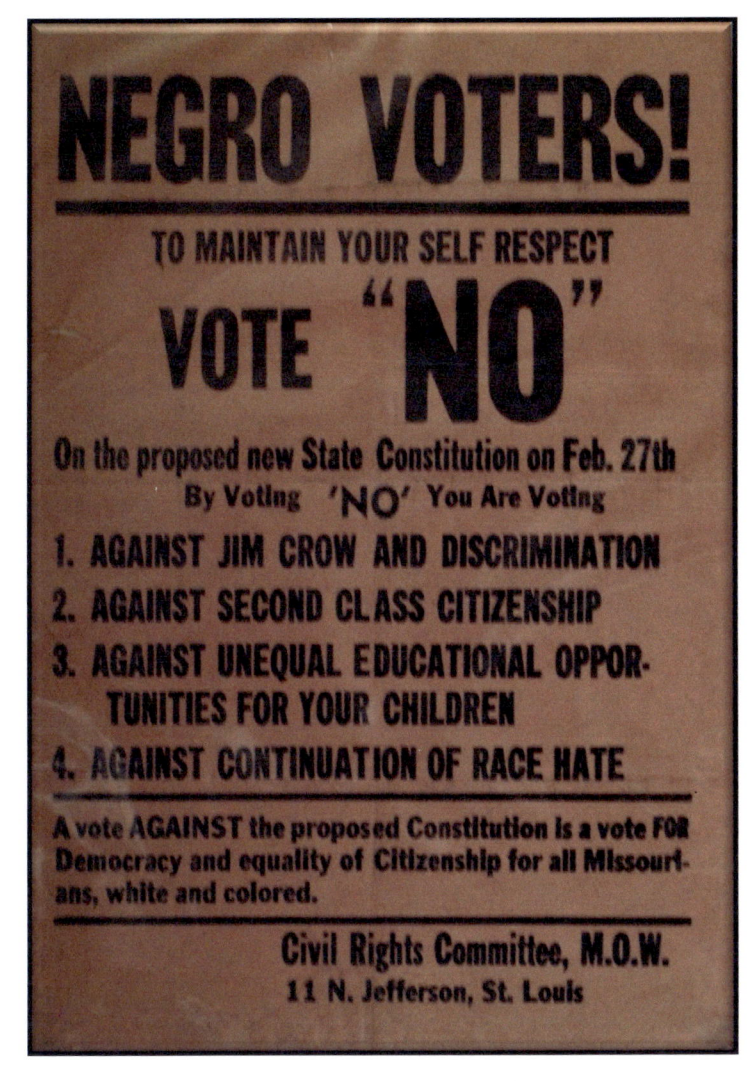

Defending Civil Rights: A Call to Action for Black Voters in Missouri

The Civil Rights Committee in St. Louis, Missouri, created this historic flyer as a call to action directed at Black voters to oppose a proposed new state constitution on February 27th.

The bold headline, "NEGRO VOTERS! TO MAINTAIN YOUR SELF RESPECT VOTE 'NO'," sets the tone for the urgent appeal. Below, it lists four key reasons to vote against the measure:
1. Against Jim Crow and discrimination.
2. Against second-class citizenship.
3. Against unequal educational opportunities for your children.
4. Against the continuation of race hate.

The flyer emphasizes that voting "NO" represents a stand for democracy, equality, and citizenship rights for all Missourians, both Black and white. It situates itself firmly within the Civil Rights Movement's struggle to dismantle institutionalized racism and segregation. The flyer reflects the grassroots organizing and activism efforts to mobilize Black voters as part of the broader fight for civil rights during this era.

Issued by the Civil Rights Committee at 11 N. Jefferson, St. Louis, this flyer serves as a powerful historical artifact of resistance against systemic oppression and the quest for racial justice.

Dr. Martin Luther King Jr.: Why I Oppose the War in Vietnam Album (1967): Highlighting his critique of U.S. militarism.

Dr. Martin Luther King, Jr. boldly criticized the United States' involvement in the Vietnam War on this powerful album, *Why I Oppose the War in Vietnam*. Released by Black Forum Records, a subsidiary of Motown dedicated to promoting Black activism and voices, the album captures King's compelling moral and political arguments delivered on April 4, 1967, at Riverside Church in New York City.

The album cover is striking, rendered in shades of blue with an evocative illustration of Dr. King passionately speaking, juxtaposed with haunting imagery of soldiers, warplanes, and the human toll of war. The bold typography emphasizes King's name and the significance of his message, further underscored by the *Black Forum* branding, symbolizing the urgency of amplifying Black perspectives on issues of justice and peace.

In this speech, Dr. King condemned the war not only as a misuse of resources that could address poverty and inequality at home but also as a moral failure that disproportionately affected the marginalized, including Black soldiers and Vietnamese civilians. By connecting the struggles of the Civil Rights Movement to global injustices, King underscored the indivisibility of justice, marking this as one of his most controversial and courageous public statements.

This album stands as a testament to Dr. King's unwavering commitment to peace and justice, revealing his role as both a civil rights leader and a global humanitarian. It remains a vital artifact of his legacy and the ongoing struggle for equity and human dignity.

Black Panther full page advertisement: Celebrating Huey P. Newton and Bobby Seale

This poster promotes the Intercommunal Day of Solidarity event for Bobby Seale, Chairman of the Black Panther Party, and a Post-Birthday Celebration for Huey P. Newton, Minister of Defense and Supreme Commander of the Black Panther Party. The event took place on Friday, March 5, 1971, at the Oakland Auditorium Arena in Oakland, California, from 7:00 PM to 11:00 PM.

The design of the poster features bold, striking typography, paired with black-and-white portraits of Bobby Seale and Huey P. Newton, symbolizing their leadership and revolutionary vision. Beneath their images, illustrations of rifles evoke the militant stance of the Black Panther Party in defending Black communities against systemic oppression and police brutality.

The event promised speeches by both Seale and Newton, along with revolutionary singing by The Lumpen, the Black Panther Party's vocal group, backed by the Freedom Messengers. The Grateful Dead and The Vanguards were also listed as performers, underscoring the event's blend of activism, culture, and solidarity.

Tickets were priced at $2.50 in advance and $3.00 at the door, with multiple community locations listed for purchasing tickets, reflecting the grassroots nature of the event and its connection to the local Black community.

This poster serves as a powerful artifact of the Black Panther Party's cultural and political activities in the 1970s, illustrating their dedication to community-building, solidarity, and the fight for racial justice.

Chairman Fred Hampton Cover of The Black Panther (1969): Honoring the revolutionary leader.

This is an issue of *The Black Panther: Black Community News Service,* published on December 13, 1969, featuring Fred Hampton, the Chairman of the Illinois chapter of the Black Panther Party, prominently on the cover. The headline memorializes Hampton's declaration, "I am a revolutionary," and notes his tragic death on December 4, 1969, labeling it as a murder by "fascist pigs." The powerful imagery and bold red tones emphasize the urgency and injustice of his assassination.

Chairman Fred Hampton was a charismatic leader and visionary whose work included community service initiatives like free breakfast programs for children and efforts to unite people across racial and class lines through the Rainbow Coalition. His killing, orchestrated by the FBI and Chicago Police Department under the COINTELPRO program, became a galvanizing event for the Black liberation movement, sparking outrage and calls for justice nationwide.

This issue highlights the aftermath of Hampton's murder, framing it as a stark example of systemic oppression against the Black Panther Party and the broader fight for racial and social justice. The content inside delves deeper into the details of Hampton's assassination and ongoing attacks on the Black Panther Party, including an exposé on the "genocide attempt" in Los Angeles. This publication serves as both a historical record of state violence and a rallying cry for continued resistance.

STOKELY CARMICHAEL FREE HUEY ALBUM (1970s): A RALLYING CRY FOR BLACK POWER.

This album cover features Stokely Carmichael (later known as Kwame Ture), a prominent civil rights activist and revolutionary, on the Black Forum Records label. The bold design reflects the spirit of Black empowerment and activism during the late 1960s and early 1970s.

The cover prominently displays Carmichael's name in large, uppercase red lettering at the top, making a statement as powerful as the man himself. Below his name, a black-and-white image of Carmichael captures him mid-speech, emphasizing his passionate oratory and leadership. The textured red background adds depth and intensity, symbolizing the fiery energy of the Black Power movement.

The slogan "FREE HUEY!" in white text with an exclamation mark highlights the struggle to free Huey P. Newton, co-founder of the Black Panther Party, who was imprisoned at the time. To the right, the vertical text "BLACK FORUM" appears in bold black lettering, emphasizing the record label's mission to amplify revolutionary voices. The Black Forum logo, positioned in the bottom right corner, reinforces its dedication to preserving and sharing messages of Black liberation and resistance.

Overall, this cover embodies the urgency and determination of the Black liberation movement, with Stokely Carmichael's powerful presence symbolizing the fight for freedom and justice.

AFENI SHAKUR COVER STORY ON RAT MAGAZINE (1971): SHOWCASING HER LEADERSHIP WITHIN THE BLACK PANTHER PARTY.

This is a cover of *RAT Subterranean News,* an underground newspaper published during the late 1960s and early 1970s. Dated February 6–23, the issue highlights a cover story on Afeni Shakur, a prominent leader of the Black Panther Party and mother of the iconic rapper Tupac Shakur. The feature focuses on Shakur's involvement in the "Panther 21" trial, a high-profile legal case in which 21 members of the Black Panther Party were accused of conspiring to commit acts of domestic terrorism in New York City.

The article includes an interview conducted by Jane Alpert, showcasing Shakur's insights on the trial, the systemic oppression faced by Black communities, and the resilience of the Panthers in the face of injustice. Her words capture her revolutionary spirit, highlighting her role as a leading voice in the struggle for civil rights and social justice.

The cover photograph, taken by Barbara Rothkrug, depicts a contemplative Shakur smoking a cigarette, symbolizing the weight of the trial and her steadfast determination. This issue of *RAT Subterranean News* represents an important moment in the history of Black resistance, documenting the Black Panther Party's efforts against systemic racism and Shakur's pivotal role within the movement.

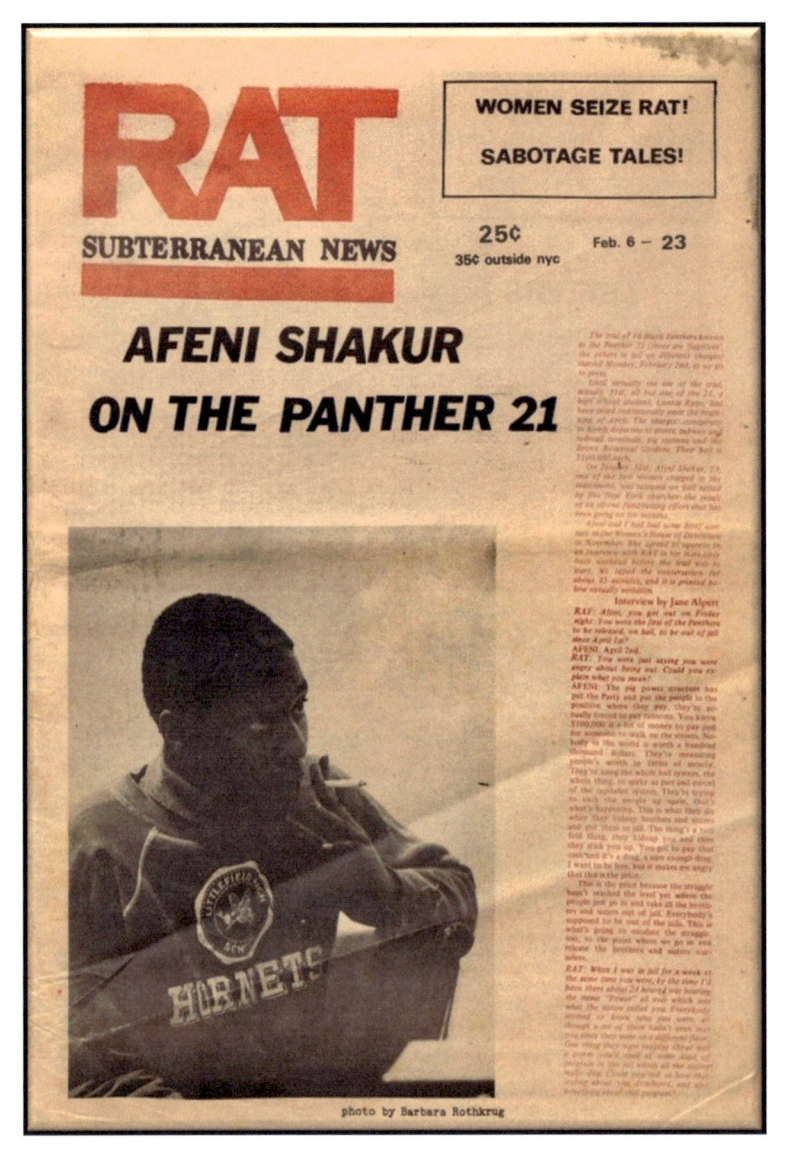

"Free the Soledad Brothers" Poster (1971): Advocating for Justice and Equity.

This powerful poster is a call to action for the release of the Soledad Brothers—George Jackson, John Clutchette, and Fleeta Drumgo—who were accused of killing a prison guard in California's Soledad Prison in 1970. The case became a symbol of racial and social injustice, sparking national and international protests led by activists, intellectuals, and organizations fighting for civil rights.

The poster features striking portraits of the three men alongside a quote from Ho Chi Minh's *Prison Diary*: *"People who come out of prison can build up the country. Misfortune is the test of the people's fidelity. Those who protest at injustice are people of true merit. When the prison doors are opened, the real dragon will fly out."*

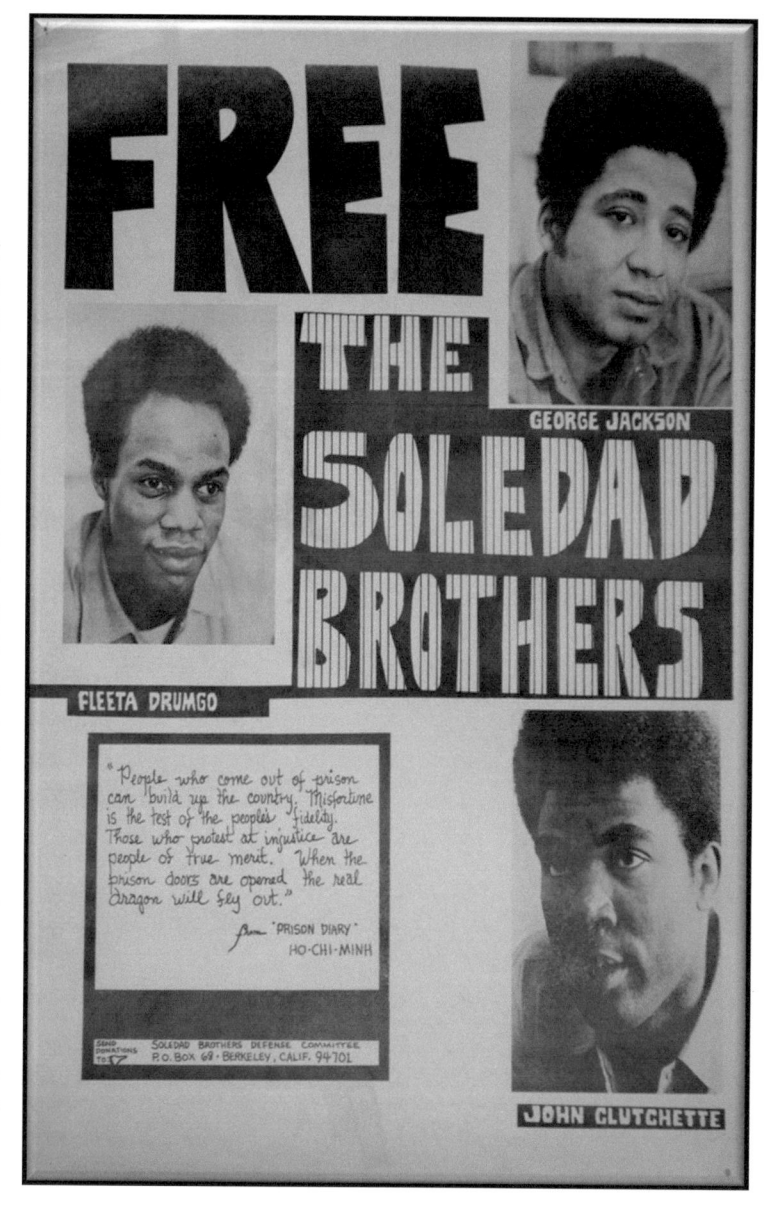

Created by the Soledad Brothers Defense Committee, this poster urged supporters to send donations to aid in their legal defense. It embodies the spirit of resistance against systemic oppression, amplifying the voices of incarcerated individuals whose cases represented broader struggles against racism, mass incarceration, and state violence. The poster remains an enduring artifact of the Black Power Movement and the fight for justice in America.

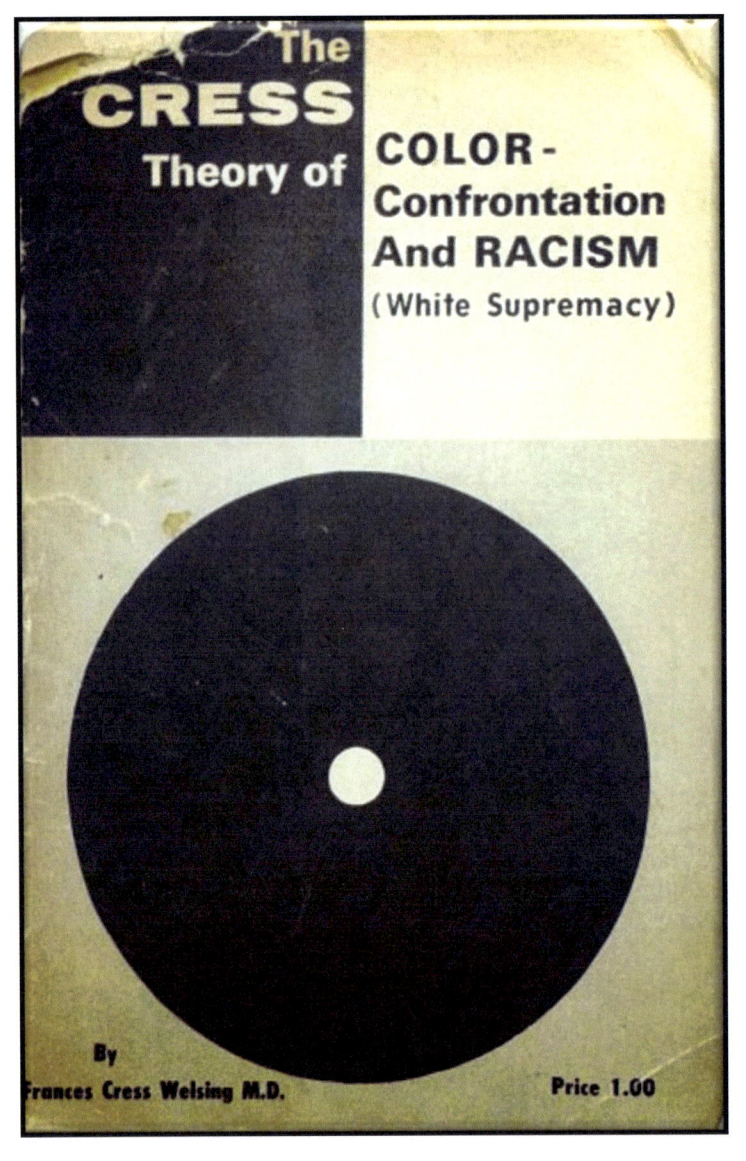

Dr. Frances Cress Welsing's Cress Theory Pamphlet (1970s): Groundbreaking work on systemic racism.

This is the first edition of the pamphlet *The Cress Theory of Color-Confrontation and Racism (White Supremacy)* by Dr. Frances Cress Welsing, published in the early 1970s. This groundbreaking work explores the psychological underpinnings of white supremacy, positing that racism stems from a deep-seated fear of genetic annihilation due to the dominance of melanin in people of color. The stark and minimalist design of the cover, featuring concentric black and white circles, symbolizes the central themes of confrontation and imbalance between racial groups.

Dr. Welsing's pamphlet was a foundational text in Black psychology, offering a bold and provocative framework for understanding systemic racism and white supremacy. It has been celebrated for its originality and for sparking vital conversations about race, power, and identity in the United States and beyond.

This text also served as the conceptual inspiration for Public Enemy's iconic 1990 album *Fear of a Black Planet*. The album's title and themes echo Dr. Welsing's theories, translating her intellectual work into a sonic manifesto for resistance and empowerment in the hip-hop era. As a result, this pamphlet not only stands as a significant piece of scholarship but also as a cultural artifact that influenced one of the most politically charged albums in music history.

MUTULU SHAKUR FBI WANTED FLYER (1982): REFLECTING GOVERNMENT SURVEILLANCE OF BLACK LEADERS.

Mutulu Shakur, an activist, acupuncturist, and freedom fighter was listed on this FBI wanted flyer as wanted for his alleged involvement in the 1981 armed robbery of a Brinks armored truck in New York. The flyer includes fingerprint records, photographs of Shakur taken in 1981 and 1982, and a detailed description of his physical appearance and aliases, including his birth name, Jeral Wayne Williams. The document cautions that Shakur was "known to associate with extremist groups" and alleged to have a "great propensity for criminal activity and violence."

Mutulu Shakur, stepfather to iconic rapper and cultural figure Tupac Shakur, was deeply involved in movements for Black liberation and social justice. He worked as an acupuncturist, co-founding health programs in underserved communities and integrating traditional healing methods with activism. Mutulu's legacy also connects to the broader struggle against systemic oppression and the criminalization of Black leaders in America.

This flyer, issued during the height of the FBI's COINTELPRO activities, reflects the intense surveillance and targeting of individuals associated with Black liberation movements. It symbolizes both the resistance of activists like Shakur and the heavy-handed responses by the federal government during this era. His case remains a potent example of the intersection of activism, family legacy, and systemic repression.

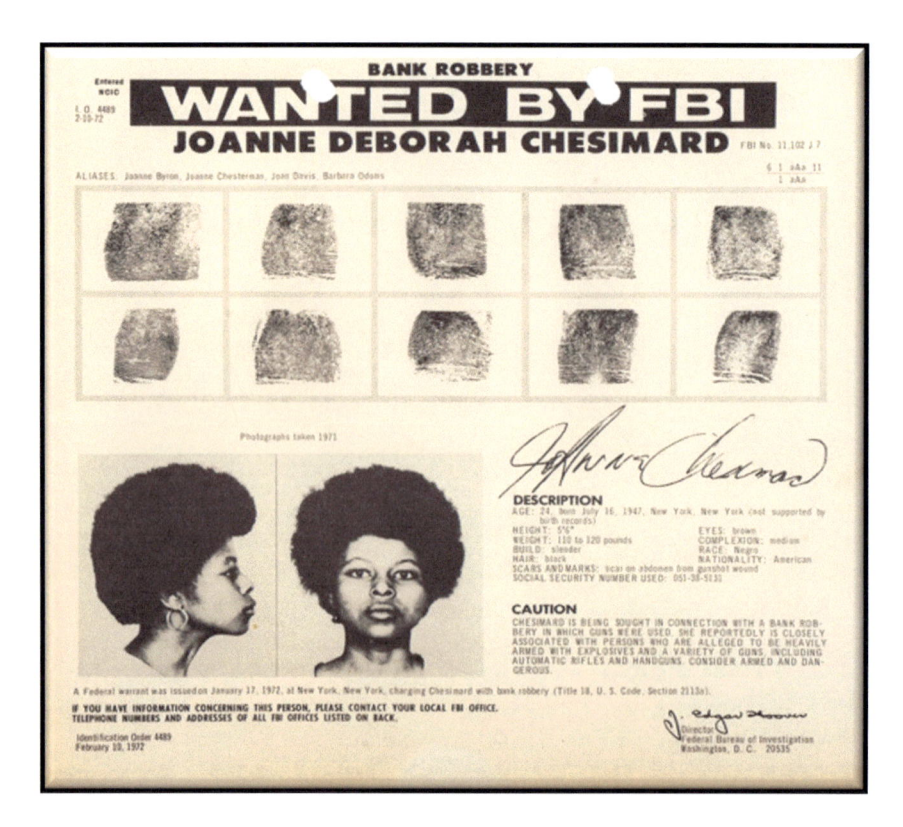

JoAnne Chesimard FBI Wanted Flyer (1972): Reflecting government surveillance of Black leaders.

The Wanted By FBI flyer for JoAnne Chesimard, also known as Assata Shakur, issued by law enforcement on February 10, 1972, features a black-and-white photograph of Chesimard alongside detailed descriptions of her physical appearance and alleged crimes. She was accused of being involved in multiple armed robberies, kidnappings, and other felonies, presenting her as a dangerous figure associated with revolutionary activities and the Black Liberation Army.

In 1977, Chesimard was convicted of the 1973 murder of a New Jersey state trooper, but in 1979, she escaped from prison with the help of armed associates, including Mutulu Shakur, a prominent figure in the Black liberation movement. Mutulu Shakur is also the stepfather of hip-hop icon Tupac Shakur, while Assata is Tupac's godmother. After her escape, she fled to Cuba, where she was granted political asylum and remains to this day. Her story has made her a polarizing figure, celebrated by some as a revolutionary symbol of resistance and condemned by others as a convicted fugitive.

Her story has inspired many artists in hip hop culture including Public Enemy, Tupac, X Clan, Digable Planets, and Common.

H. Rap Brown FBI Wanted Flyer (1970): Said, "Violence is American as Cherry Pie".

    This Wanted By FBI flyer features Imam Jamil Al-Amin, better known as H. Rap Brown, a prominent civil rights activist and leader in the Black Power movement. The flyer, issued on May 5, 1970, charges Al-Amin with interstate flight, arson, inciting to riot, and failure to appear. It includes Brown's aliases, fingerprints, and photographs taken in 1967, along with detailed physical descriptions such as his height (6'3"), weight (180-185 pounds), and distinctive physical features.

    H. Rap Brown, born on October 4, 1943, in Baton Rouge, Louisiana, was a fiery orator and former chairman of the Student Nonviolent Coordinating Committee (SNCC), later aligning with the Black Panther Party. Known for his uncompromising rhetoric on racial justice and self-determination, Brown became a polarizing figure in the civil rights era. The flyer highlights Brown's previous convictions for firearms violations and labels him as armed and dangerous, reinforcing the FBI's narrative of him as a threat to national security.

    The document reflects the era's broader context, when the FBI, under COINTELPRO, targeted prominent Black activists to suppress the growing momentum of the civil rights and Black Power movements. Flyers like this one served not only as a law enforcement tool but also as propaganda to delegitimize activists and stoke public fear. This artifact exemplifies the systemic efforts to criminalize resistance and dissent during a time of profound social change. It remains a testament to the tension between state power and grassroots movements for racial equity and justice.

**SISTER SOULJAH FLYER AT WAYNE STATE UNIVERSITY (2000):
HIGHLIGHTING HER ACTIVISM AND LITERARY CONTRIBUTIONS.**

Wayne State University's chapter of the NAACP hosted a speaking engagement featuring Sister Souljah as part of their Women's History Month celebration on Saturday, March 4, 2000. The event, titled "Finding Our Power," was held at the Community Arts Auditorium on campus at 6 PM and was free and open to the public. Sister Souljah, a renowned activist, author, and hip-hop artist, is celebrated for her thought-provoking commentary on racial, social, and economic justice. This event aimed to inspire and empower attendees while commemorating the achievements and contributions of women throughout history. The flyer reflects the significance of Sister Souljah's voice in advocating for empowerment and community action.

MARCH ON WASHINGTON PENNANT (1963): A KEEPSAKE FROM MLK'S ICONIC SPEECH.

This pennant is a commemorative artifact from the historic March on Washington for Jobs and Freedom, held on August 28, 1963, in Washington, D.C. The blue felt pennant features bold white text reading: "I WAS THERE NATIONAL MARCH FOR FREEDOM AUG. 28, 1963 WASHINGTON, D.C." It's simple yet striking design reflects the gravity and significance of the event.

The March on Washington was a pivotal moment in the Civil Rights Movement, drawing over 250,000 people to advocate for civil and economic rights for African Americans. This event is famously remembered for Dr. Martin Luther King Jr.'s "I Have a Dream" speech, which articulated a powerful vision for racial equality and justice in America.

This pennant serves as a tangible reminder of the courage and solidarity of those who participated in the march. It symbolizes not only the collective struggle for equality but also the personal pride of those who stood on the frontlines of the fight for civil rights. As an artifact, it offers a unique glimpse into the ways attendees memorialized their presence at this historic event.

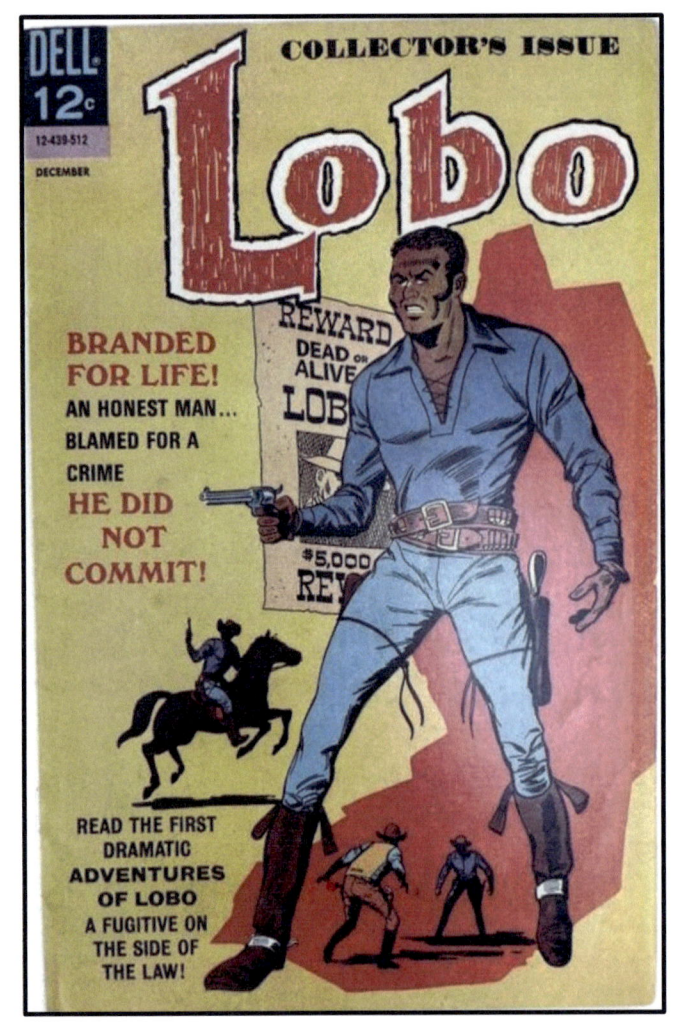

Lobo Comic Book (December, Dell Comics): A Groundbreaking Piece of History

This December issue of *Lobo*, published by Dell Comics in 1965, represents a milestone in comic book history as it features the first Black cowboy hero to star in his own comic series. The cover highlights Lobo, a strong and noble figure, branded as an outlaw for a crime he did not commit. The tagline, "Branded for life! An honest man…blamed for a crime he did not commit!" sets the tone for his dramatic adventures as a fugitive seeking justice while standing on the side of the law.

Lobo was groundbreaking in its time for presenting a Black hero in the lead role during the height of the Civil Rights Movement, challenging prevailing racial stereotypes in popular media. The character's depiction as a moral, intelligent, and heroic figure marked a bold step forward in diversifying the comic book landscape, paving the way for future representation of Black characters in mainstream media.

However, the series faced challenges in the marketplace, reflecting the racial tensions of the era. Reports suggest that some vendors returned the comic unopened, demonstrating the resistance to a Black hero in a predominantly white entertainment industry. As a result, *Lobo* only lasted two issues, making this artifact a rare and significant collector's item.

Today, *Lobo* is celebrated for its cultural and historical importance, symbolizing a turning point in the fight for racial equality in popular culture and inspiring the creation of more diverse and inclusive heroes in the years that followed.

**MILLION MAN MARCH BUMPER STICKER AND BUTTONS (1995):
SYMBOLIZING UNITY AND MASS ACTION.**

The "I WAS THERE" bumper sticker and buttons commemorate the historic Million Man March, held on October 16, 1995, in Washington, D.C. These mementos embody the pride and profound significance of this transformative event. Organized by Minister Louis Farrakhan and the Nation of Islam, the Million Man March was a call to action for unity, atonement, and empowerment among African American men. This monumental gathering far exceeded its original goal, bringing nearly two million men to the National Mall to address critical issues such as social justice, racial equality, and community accountability. These artifacts stand as powerful symbols of the solidarity, purpose, and historic impact of that day.

GANDHI, KING, IKEDA PEACE AWARD MEDAL (2004): HONORING LERONE BENNETT

This medal, awarded to editor and historian Lerone Bennett Jr. in 2004, represents the Gandhi, King, Ikeda Peace Award, an honor celebrating individuals whose lives and work embody the principles of peace, nonviolence, and social justice. The medal features the profiles of three global icons: Mahatma Gandhi, Dr. Martin Luther King Jr., and Daisaku Ikeda, symbolizing their shared commitment to peace, human dignity, and interfaith understanding.

Lerone Bennett Jr., a renowned historian, author, and editor of *Ebony* magazine, received this prestigious award for his lifelong dedication to chronicling African American history and advocating for social justice. Through groundbreaking works such as *Before the Mayflower: A History of Black America* and his role in shaping cultural and political discourse, Bennett used his platform to amplify the struggles and triumphs of Black Americans while promoting the ideals of equity and nonviolence.

This medal serves as a testament to Bennett's significant contributions to the global pursuit of justice and peace, placing him in the lineage of transformative leaders who have inspired change through their words and actions.

Chapter 3

SOUNDWAVES OF CHANGE: THE POWER OF BLACK EXPRESSION

This section captures the vital role of Black voices in resistance and liberation. Whether through music, comedy, spoken word, or activism, Black creators and leaders have used their platforms to amplify voices, inspire change, and challenge oppression. This section broadens the lens to include not only music but also the cultural, political, and artistic contributions that have driven social transformation. The artifacts showcased here embody the resilience, creativity, and determination of individuals who dared to speak out, laugh in the face of adversity, and push boundaries.

This collection spans the spectrum of Black expression, from the spoken word recordings of *Guess Who's Coming Home*, capturing the reflections of Black soldiers in Vietnam, to the political wit of Redd Foxx, whose comedy bridged entertainment and cultural critique. Flyers and posters highlight not only musicians but also activists like Stokely Carmichael, whose fiery rhetoric transformed words into weapons for revolution. "Our grandfathers had to run, run, run. My generation's out of breath. We ain't running no more," Carmichael declared, a sentiment that reverberates through the unapologetic art and activism of his era.

Artifacts such as DJ Kool Herc's belt buckle and Afrika Islam's Zulu Nation jacket represent hip-hop's emergence as a cultural movement that blended music, fashion, and activism. Meanwhile, magazine covers featuring figures like Michael Jackson and Treach reflect the broader cultural impact of Black artists who transcended their mediums to become symbols of creativity and empowerment.

At its core, this section showcases how Black expression has fueled resistance and transformation. From revolutionary concert flyers to spoken word albums, these artifacts remind us that expression is not just a reflection of the times but a driving force in shaping them. As Fred Hampton once said, "You can kill a revolutionary, but you can't kill the revolution," and the works displayed here prove that Black voices in all their forms—music, comedy, or activism—continue to inspire generations in the fight for justice and liberation.

Expression has always been a cornerstone of Black resistance and liberation. Whether through music, comedy, spoken word, or activism, Black creators and leaders have used their platforms to amplify voices, inspire change, and challenge oppression. This section showcases artifacts that embody the resilience, creativity, and determination of individuals who dared to speak out, laugh in the face of adversity, and push boundaries.

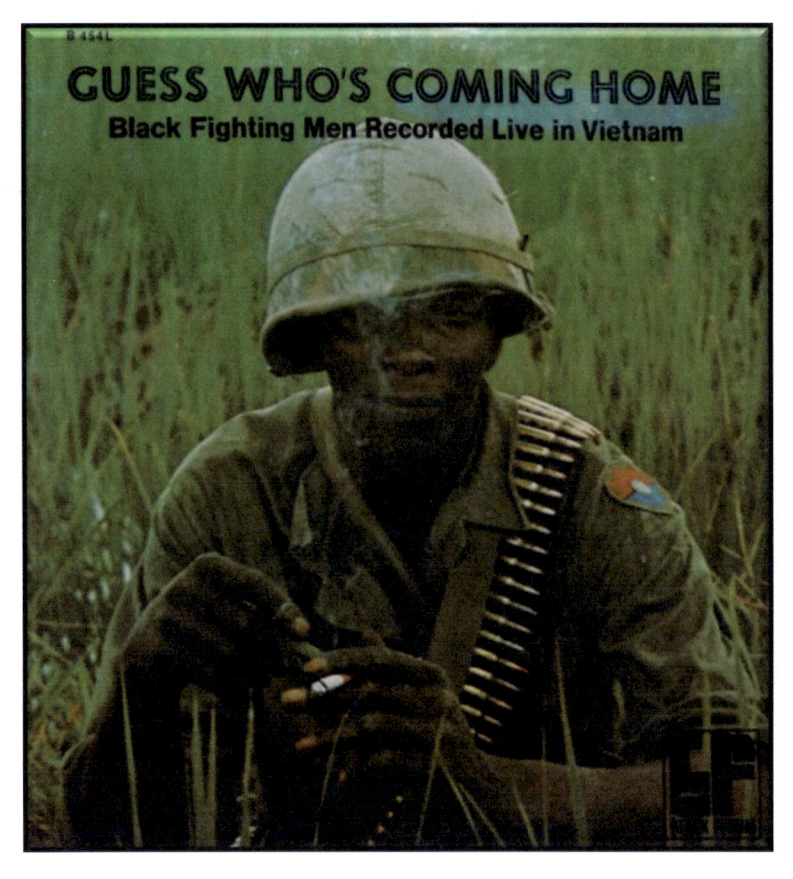

Guess Who's Coming Home Album (Vietnam War Era): Amplifying Black soldiers' voices.

"Guess Who's Coming Home: Black Fighting Men Recorded Live in Vietnam," is a rare and poignant document of African American soldiers' experiences during the Vietnam War. Released by Motown's Black Forum label, this album captures the voices of Black servicemen sharing their thoughts, emotions, and reflections while serving in one of the most controversial wars in American history.

The cover features a striking image of a Black soldier in full combat gear, sitting amidst the dense greenery of Vietnam, smoking a cigarette. The soldier's expression conveys resilience, exhaustion, and contemplation, embodying the complex realities faced by Black men fighting in a foreign land while confronting systemic racism at home.

This record stands as both an oral history and a cultural artifact, providing an unfiltered glimpse into the lives of soldiers who often found themselves doubly burdened—fighting not only for their country but also for civil rights and recognition within it. The album amplifies the voices of those who were often overlooked in mainstream narratives about the war, making it an essential piece of historical and cultural significance.

Motown's Black Forum label, known for its politically charged releases, aimed to spotlight the struggles and resilience of African Americans during turbulent times. This album is a powerful reminder of the sacrifices made by Black soldiers and their enduring contributions to history, even under the weight of oppression and inequity.

Sir Nose D'Voidoffunk Poster: Representing Parliament Funkadelic's artistic influence.

George Clinton's character Sir Nose D'Voidoffunk featured on this promotional poster is a recurring figure in the mythology of Parliament-Funkadelic's musical universe. Illustrated by Pedro Bell, the iconic artist behind much of Parliament-Funkadelic's visual identity, this poster showcases his signature surreal and psychedelic style. The artwork is dominated by vibrant shades of pink, orange, and red, capturing the playful yet profound aesthetic of P-Funk.

Sir Nose is depicted as a lanky, exaggerated figure with a large nose, dressed in a sleek suit and cape, embodying a villainous, yet comical persona. The starburst over his eye and his outstretched finger add a theatrical flair, emphasizing his role as an antagonist to the funk movement led by George Clinton's Dr. Funkenstein. The stylized clouds at the bottom of the poster create a fantastical, otherworldly setting, underscoring the cosmic funk mythology that defined Parliament-Funkadelic's creative vision.

Pedro Bell's distinctive touch is evident in the bold composition and intricate details, blending Afro-futurism, humor, and social commentary into the design. This poster reflects the visual storytelling central to P-Funk's albums and performances, where characters like Sir Nose represented the anti-funk resistance, an enemy of groove and rhythm. As a promotional artifact, this poster serves as a cultural emblem of the funk era's creativity, theatricality, and defiance of musical and social norms. Bell's contribution solidifies it as a masterwork of funk mythology.

DJ KOOL HERC'S BELT BUCKLE: PERSONAL ACCESSORY OF HIP-HOP'S FOUNDER.

This belt buckle belonged to DJ Kool Herc, widely regarded as the father of hip-hop. The buckle is a bold and vibrant accessory, featuring a large metal design with a central green star surrounded by red, yellow, and green embellishments, evoking the colors of Rastafarian and Pan-African pride. The craftsmanship and colorful detailing reflect Herc's connection to his Jamaican roots and the cultural influences that shaped the early hip-hop movement.

The leather belt itself is customized with the name "KOOL" prominently embossed, adding a personal touch that signifies Herc's identity as a pioneering figure in the genre. This belt buckle is not merely a piece of fashion but a symbol of Herc's individuality and the style that defined the hip-hop scene of the 1970s.

As a physical artifact, this buckle is a testament to Kool Herc's pivotal role in the birth of hip-hop culture, where his groundbreaking DJ techniques at Bronx parties in the early 1970s laid the foundation for a global movement. It serves as a tangible reminder of his enduring legacy and influence on music, fashion, and cultural expression.

Afrika Islam's Zulu Nation Jacket: Showcasing Pan-African pride in hip-hop.

This distinctive jacket belonged to hip-hop DJ Afrika Islam, a prominent member of the Zulu Nation and pioneer of hip-hop culture. The jacket features a bold black-and-white cowhide pattern, emblematic of the unique and expressive style associated with early hip-hop fashion. It prominently displays several embroidered patches that reflect Afrika Islam's affiliations and contributions to the movement.

On the back, the jacket features a striking patch in the shape of the African continent, embroidered with the text "Afrika Islam" and "Rhyme Syndicate", underscoring his connection to the collective led by Ice-T and the broader mission of hip-hop as a platform for unity and expression. The crescent and star within the African map symbolize ties to Afrocentric and Islamic influences within the Zulu Nation's ideology.

On the front, a colorful Zulu Nation patch is prominently displayed, reaffirming his membership in the influential organization founded by Afrika Bambaataa. This collective played a crucial role in establishing hip-hop's cultural and political foundation, emphasizing knowledge, unity, and social empowerment.

This jacket is not only a bold fashion statement but also a significant artifact of hip-hop history, representing Afrika Islam's role in shaping the genre's music, style, and cultural ethos. It encapsulates the individuality and collective identity of the hip-hop movement during its formative years.

Hip-Hop Benefit Flyer Featuring Mr. Magic, Melle Mel, and DJ Kool Herc: A lineup of early hip-hop legends.

This vibrant hip-hop flyer advertises a star-studded benefit event for the Fourth Wall Repertory Company, showcasing some of the biggest legends in the hip-hop world. Headlined by WBLS's Mr. Magic, a pioneering hip-hop radio DJ, the event features guest star Melle Mel, the iconic frontman of Grandmaster Flash and the Furious Five, whose socially conscious lyrics helped define early hip-hop.

Supporting acts include DJ Kool Herc, widely regarded as the father of hip-hop, D.ST. (best known for his groundbreaking turntable work on Herbie Hancock's "Rockit"), Brother D, and Kid Nice, all contributing to a lineup that reflects the dynamic and influential voices of hip-hop's golden era. The flyer also highlights a performance by Oedipus, representing Boston's WBCN radio, broadening the event's cultural reach.

The bold, eye-catching design features a photo of Melle Mel flexing his arms, embodying the strength and energy of hip-hop culture. The vivid red, green, and black color scheme emphasizes the event's connection to the community and the broader social movements supported by hip-hop.

Taking place on Saturday, August 9 at the Fourth Wall Theater in New York City, this benefit captures the spirit of early hip-hop as both a cultural force and a platform for activism, celebrating the genre's ability to inspire and support creative and social causes.

MERRY X-MAS CELEBRATION FLYER FEATURING MC SHA ROCK AND THE FUNKY 4+1 (1980): CELEBRATING THE FIRST FEMALE MC.

This is a flyer for a Merry X-Mas Celebration held on Friday, December 19, 1980, featuring some of the earliest pioneers of hip-hop culture. The event headlined DJ Breakout & The Funky 4 + 1, including groundbreaking members like MC Sha Rock, recognized as the first female MC in hip-hop. Sha Rock's influence in the hip-hop community has extended into modern times, as she continues to inspire audiences through events like her tours with the Black History 101 Mobile Museum.

The flyer also showcases other notable acts such as K. Connection, Kenny Ken, Gregski, and Serious 3 Doc "La Rock", along with DJs and MCs like M&M, EZ Mike, Paradise, and others. These performers represent the vibrant, formative era of hip-hop, where local jams served as incubators for the culture's growth.

The hand-drawn illustration on the flyer features a sharply dressed cartoon cat strolling over an urban landscape, capturing the playful, grassroots aesthetic of early hip-hop events. The creative typography and community-focused design highlight the DIY approach that defined the culture during its early days.

Held at the James Monroe Center, with an entry fee of just $2 for ladies and $3 for men, the event embodies the accessible and communal nature of early hip-hop jams. This flyer stands as an artifact of hip-hop's rich history, showcasing the movement's pioneers and their enduring cultural legacy.

Fresh Fest Poster (1980s): Marking hip-hop's rise to national prominence.

The *Swatch Watch NYC Fresh Festival* was one of the first major hip-hop tours in history, highlighting the growing prominence of hip-hop culture during the 1980s. Sponsored by Swatch Watch, the festival took place at the Oakland Coliseum Arena on Sunday, December 9, with performances scheduled for both 2:30 PM and 8:00 PM. The lineup featured some of the most influential pioneers of hip-hop: Run D.M.C., Kurtis Blow, Whodini, The Fat Boys, Newcleus among some incredible breakers.

This festival represents a pivotal moment in hip-hop history, showcasing the genre's transition from local block parties to large-scale national tours. By sponsoring the event, Swatch Watch demonstrated hip-hop's increasing commercial viability and cultural impact. The NYC Fresh Fest is remembered as a landmark in solidifying hip-hop's place in the broader music and entertainment industry.

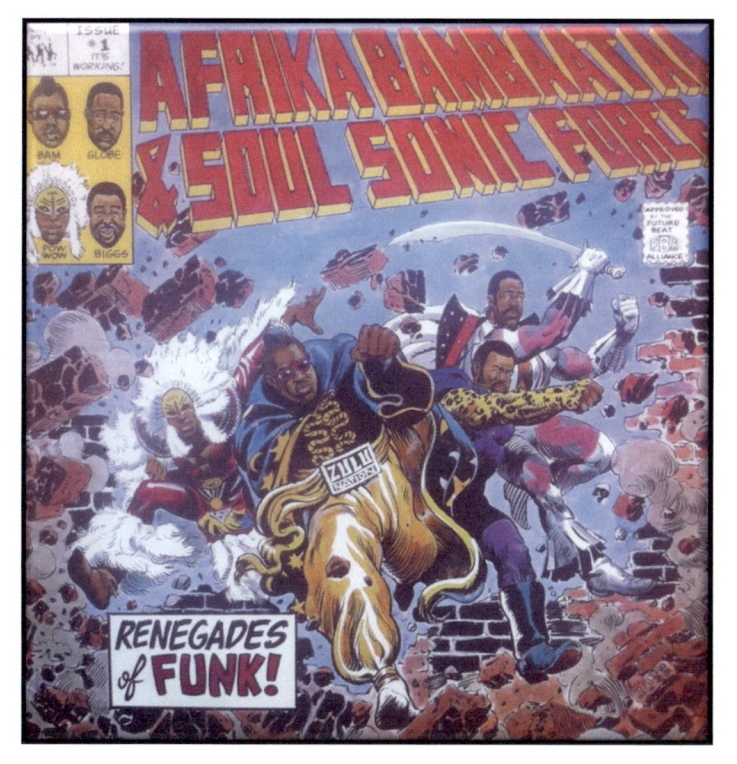

RENEGADES OF FUNK ALBUM BY AFRIKA BAMBAATAA & SOUL SONIC FORCE: MELDING FUNK AND SOCIAL CONSCIOUSNESS.

This album cover for *Renegades of Funk* by Afrika Bambaataa & Soul Sonic Force is a vibrant and iconic piece of visual storytelling that encapsulates the revolutionary spirit of early hip-hop and electro-funk. The cover, designed like a comic book, features the group members—Afrika Bambaataa, Pow Wow, G.L.O.B.E., and Biggs—portrayed as larger-than-life superheroes bursting through a crumbling brick wall. Their dynamic poses and bold costumes emphasize their roles as cultural disruptors and pioneers of the hip-hop movement.

Afrika Bambaataa, adorned with a cape and "Zulu Nation" emblem, stands at the forefront, symbolizing his leadership in the Universal Zulu Nation, an organization that fused hip-hop culture with social awareness and activism. The explosive imagery, paired with the title *Renegades of Funk,* reflects the group's mission to challenge norms and create music that is both innovative and socially conscious.

Released in 1983, *Renegades of Funk* was a groundbreaking track that merged the burgeoning hip-hop sound with electro-funk, paving the way for future genres and influencing generations of artists. The bold typography, comic-style artwork, and the slogan "Issue #1 It's Working!" make the cover not just an album art but a manifesto for the power of funk, rhythm, and revolutionary music.

This album and its artwork remain a testament to the energy, creativity, and impact of Afrika Bambaataa and the Soul Sonic Force on music and culture.

BUDDY ESQUIRE HIP-HOP FLYER: A VISUALLY DYNAMIC ARTIFACT OF HIP-HOP CULTURE.

Buddy Esquire was one of the most iconic and influential flyer designers of the early hip-hop era. Known as the "King of the Flyer," Buddy Esquire's work set the standard for visual aesthetics in the burgeoning hip-hop movement during the late 1970s and early 1980s.

The flyer boldly proclaims "The King of the Flyer STILL IS... Buddy Esquire," emphasizing his mastery and reputation within the hip-hop community. The central artwork features a highly detailed robotic figure, blending sci-fi themes with urban culture—a hallmark of Buddy Esquire's ability to merge street style with futuristic, aspirational elements. The black-and-white design is crisp, dynamic, and visually striking, showcasing his impeccable skill in typography, composition, and illustration.

Below the artwork, tear-off tabs include his name and contact information, inviting promoters and event organizers to commission his services for flyers and more. This design not only advertises Buddy Esquire's talents but also embodies the DIY and entrepreneurial spirit of the early hip-hop scene. His work was instrumental in shaping the visual identity of hip-hop events, cementing his legacy as a pioneer in the cultural and artistic evolution of the genre.

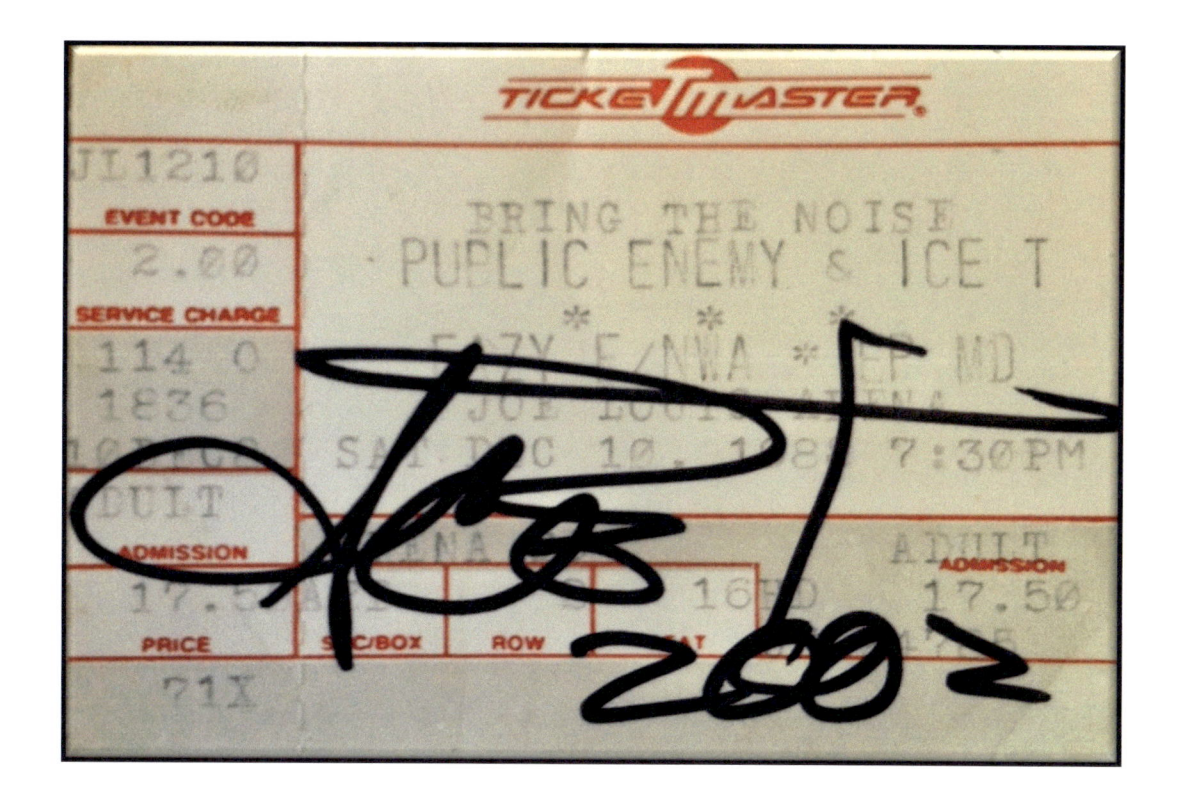

PUBLIC ENEMY AND ICE-T CONCERT TICKET STUB (1988)

The "Bring the Noise" concert featuring legendary hip-hop acts Public Enemy and Ice-T, along with additional performers Eazy-E, N.W.A., and EPMD took place on December 10, 1988 at Joe Louis Arena in Detroit. The event represents a key moment in hip-hop history, showcasing the raw energy and revolutionary messages of these influential artists during the golden age of hip-hop.

The ticket stub is prominently autographed by rapper and actor Ice-T. He signed it several years later after a speaking engagement at Wayne State University. I just so happened to be sitting next to his then girlfriend, future wife Coco. We started a conversation, and she introduced me to him after his lecture and he signed a stack of Ice T material for the museum.

This signed ticket stub captures the cultural and historical significance of the tour, which brought together some of the most politically charged and impactful voices in hip-hop. It serves as a tangible reminder of a transformative period in music, when artists used their platforms to address social issues and challenge the status quo, creating a legacy that continues to influence the genre today.

78

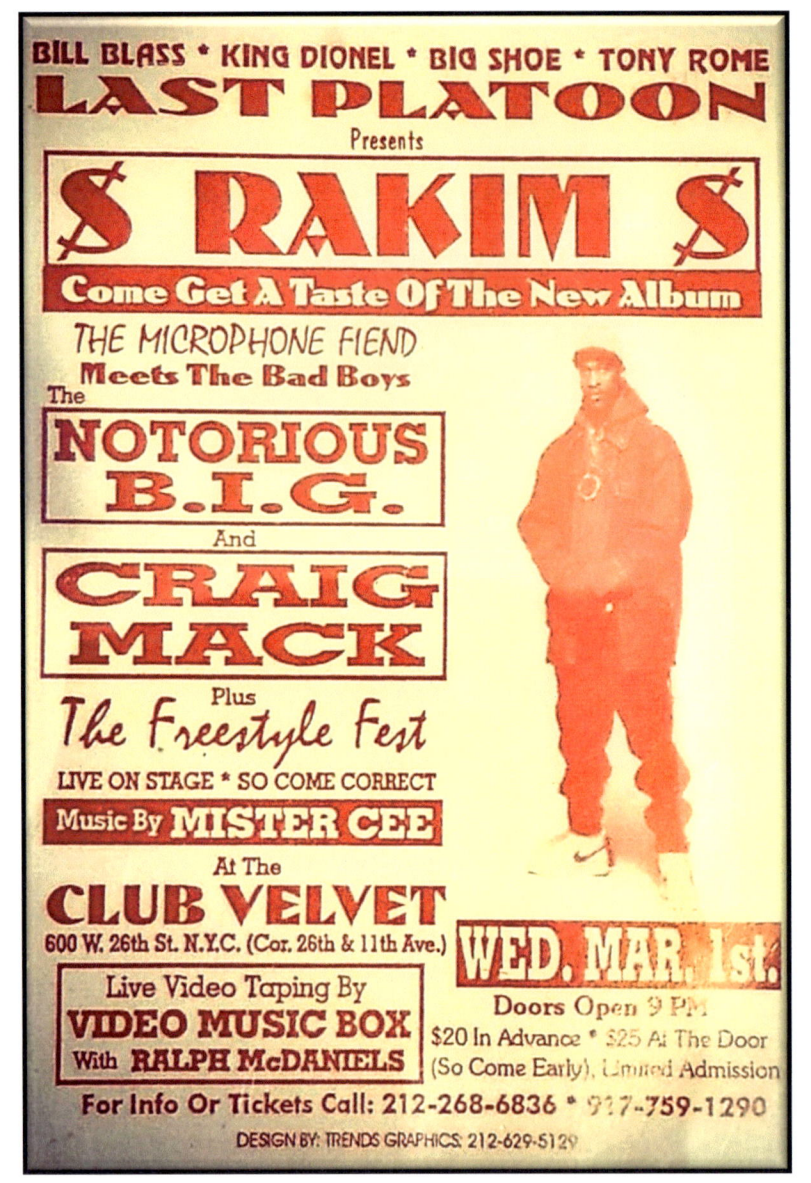

RAKIM HIP-HOP FLYER WITH NOTORIOUS B.I.G.: REPRESENTING THE GOLDEN AGE OF HIP-HOP.

This hip-hop flyer promotes an electrifying event headlined by the legendary Rakim, "The Microphone Fiend," showcasing his new album release. Billed as a powerhouse lineup, the event features groundbreaking performances from rising stars of the time, The Notorious B.I.G. and Craig Mack, marking a pivotal moment in hip-hop history as these artists gained momentum in the industry.

The event, titled *The Freestyle Fest,* promises an unforgettable evening of live music and lyrical mastery, with DJ Mister Cee providing beats for the night. The venue is Club Velvet, located at 600 W. 26th Street in New York City, scheduled for Wednesday, March 1st. Doors open at 9 PM, with tickets priced at $20 in advance and $25 at the door.

Additionally, the event includes live video taping by *Video Music Box* with Ralph McDaniels, cementing its cultural significance and archiving its impact on the hip-hop scene. Designed by Trends Graphics, this flyer captures the raw energy and excitement of the golden era of hip-hop, as iconic names like Rakim, Biggie Smalls, and Craig Mack shared the stage in an intimate yet unforgettable setting.

PHOTO OF TUPAC SHAKUR BY ERNIE PANICCIOLI: Capturing the Spirit of a Hip-Hop Revolutionary

This photograph of Tupac Shakur, captured by my dear friend and legendary photographer Ernie Paniccioli, is one of the most iconic images of Tupac. Dressed in a green utility vest with a backward cap and gold chain, he stands against a vibrant graffiti backdrop, exuding the energy, confidence, and charisma that made him a global cultural icon. The imagery, with its bold colors and street aesthetic, reflects the essence of hip-hop.

Ernie Paniccioli has been a close friend and an invaluable supporter of the Black History 101 Mobile Museum. His ability to document hip-hop culture through his lens is unparalleled, and his work goes far beyond photography—it's storytelling at its finest. This photograph is a prime example of how Ernie's artistry captures not just the image but the spirit of his subjects. Tupac's defiant stance and piercing gaze speak volumes about his connection to the culture and his role as a voice for the voiceless.

I've been fortunate to have Ernie as a collaborator and a supporter of the museum. Over the years, he has generously donated rare photographs and artifacts that have significantly enriched our collection. His contributions have been instrumental in helping us educate audiences about the global impact of Black culture and resistance. What's more, our friendship is built on a shared passion for preserving and celebrating the legacy of our people.

This photograph isn't just about Tupac—it represents the intersection of art, culture, and activism. It stands as a testament to the power of hip-hop to inspire and transform, and it reflects the enduring importance of documenting our stories. For me, it also serves as a personal reminder of the incredible bond I share with Ernie and the work we've done together to keep Black history alive and thriving for future generations.

80

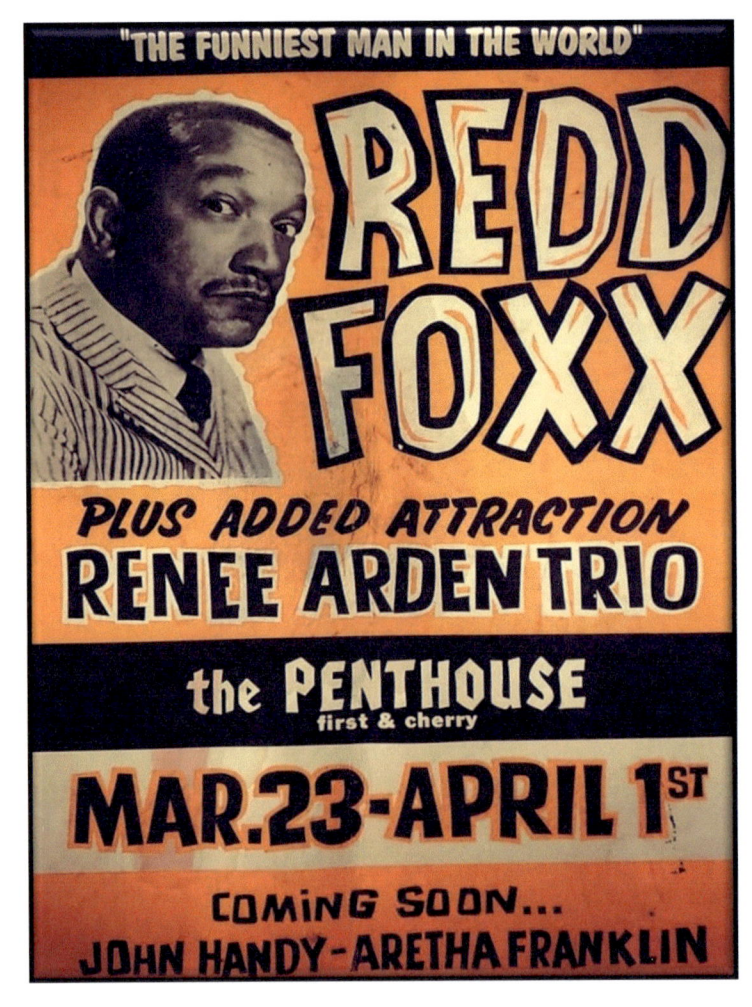

REDD FOXX CONCERT POSTER WITH ARETHA FRANKLIN (1960S): HIGHLIGHTING BLACK ENTERTAINMENT EXCELLENCE.

    The legendary comedian Redd Foxx celebrated as "The Funniest Man in the World" is featured on this vintage poster advertises a live performance scheduled to take place at *The Penthouse* located at First & Cherry from March 23 to April 1. Alongside Foxx, the poster highlights an added musical attraction, the Renee Arden Trio.

    The poster also teases upcoming performances, notably featuring the iconic Aretha Franklin and jazz saxophonist John Handy, promising audiences more unforgettable nights at the venue. The bright orange and black color scheme and bold typography capture the vibrant energy of the era, showcasing a pivotal moment in entertainment history when comedy and music were at the heart of cultural expression. Redd Foxx's name dominates the design, reflecting his star power even before his later fame on television with *Sanford and Son*.

Apollo Theater Poster: Celebrating the Icons of Soul and R&B

The legendary Apollo Theater on 125th Street in Harlem advertises a week-long showcase on this vintage poster beginning Friday, April 17th. The event, titled Jocko's Rocket Ship Revue, featured a powerhouse lineup of 1960s musical greats. Headlining the show were The Temptations, one of Motown's most iconic groups known for their smooth harmonies and timeless hits like "My Girl." Joining them were The Marvelettes, Motown's first successful girl group, celebrated for songs like "Please Mr. Postman," and Dee Clark, renowned for his soulful ballad "Raindrops."

Other notable acts included the Blue Notes, an influential R&B group later associated with Harold Melvin and Teddy Pendergrass; Donnie Elbert, a soulful crooner with a string of hits; and the Reuben Phillips Band, providing live instrumental energy throughout the performances. The poster also highlights the Apollo's famous midweek Amateur Night and a special Saturday midnight show, staples of the theater's legacy in discovering and celebrating rising talent.

Boldly designed in red and blue lettering, this poster encapsulates the energy and excitement of the Apollo Theater, a historic venue that served as a cultural cornerstone for Black music, entertainment, and artistry. It is a testament to the thriving soul and R&B scenes of the 1960s, capturing a moment when these legendary artists graced the stage of one of the most iconic theaters in the world.

Ike and Tina Turner Performance Contract: economic and cultural empowerment

This is a performance contract issued by the Spud "Nik" Booking Agency of Los Angeles, California, dated August 23, 1966, for an engagement featuring Tina Turner and the Ikettes. The contract stipulates a performance at Phelps Lounge in Detroit, Michigan, on Saturday, November 12, 1966, from 9:30 PM to 2:00 AM, with the agreed-upon wage being a $245 guarantee for the evening.

The contract is prominently marked with a red stamp reading: "THIS CONTRACT VOID WITHOUT TINA TURNER AND IKETTES", emphasizing the centrality of the act to the agreement. The document also includes the standard terms and conditions for the employment of musicians, detailing technical requirements such as a P.A. system, two microphones, and one piano tuned to A 440 pitch.

The contract is signed by representatives from both the venue and the booking agency, including Elliott Fields of Phelps Lounge as the employer and Miss Henry Ann Cain, likely representing the Spud "Nik" Booking Agency, as the booking agent.

This contract serves as a historical artifact of the mid-20th-century live music industry, showcasing the logistical and contractual details behind the performances of iconic artists like Tina Turner during her early career. It also reflects the growing influence of R&B music in venues like Detroit's Phelps Lounge, a hub for Black music and culture in the 1960s.

WHITING AUDITORIUM CONCERT POSTER: A CELEBRATION OF MOTOWN'S GOLDEN ERA

The Motor City Memories Revue was held on Saturday, September 6th, at the Whiting Auditorium in Flint, Michigan. The show featured an all-star Motown lineup, including Jr. Walker and the All Stars ("Shotgun," "What Does It Take"), Mary Wells ("My Guy," "Two Lovers"), The Contours ("Do You Love Me," "Shake Sherry"), Marv Johnson ("Move Two Mountains," "You Got What It Takes"), and The Velvelettes ("He Was Really Saying Something," "Needle in a Haystack").

The Velvelettes, a group of college students from Western Michigan University, brought youthful energy and unforgettable harmonies to the Motown scene. I was honored to have Barbee McNeil and Cal Street of The Velvelettes as guest speakers at Kalamazoo College during the Black History 101 Mobile Museum's visit. During this event, they signed this historic poster, reflecting their connection to Motown's legacy and their enduring impact on American music history.

A Style as Bold as the Sound: James Brown's Signature Suit

Once owned by the legendary James Brown this elegant suit showcases the unmistakable flair and charisma of the Godfather of Soul. Tailored to perfection, the inside of the jacket bears Brown's name embroidered as a mark of its unique provenance. Known for his electrifying performances and impeccable style, James Brown's stage presence extended beyond his music to his iconic wardrobe, making pieces like this a testament to his larger-than-life persona.

As Brown famously said, *"Hair's like a suit. You wear it. You gotta look good in it."* This philosophy extended to his fashion choices, where every outfit reflected his belief in the power of presentation and self-expression. A tangible connection to one of the most transformative figures in American music history, this suit serves as a reminder of James Brown's enduring legacy as a trendsetter and innovator.

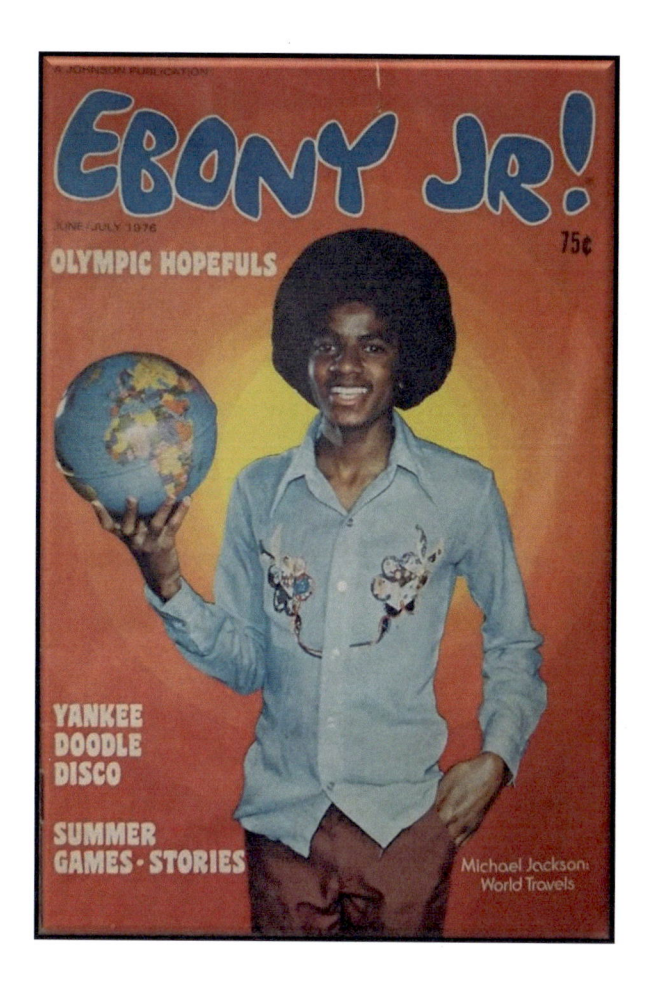

EBONY JR! COVER WITH MICHAEL JACKSON (1976): FEATURING JACKSON'S EARLY ROLE AS A YOUTH ICON.

    This is the June/July 1976 issue of *Ebony Jr!* magazine, a publication targeted at young readers and part of the Johnson Publications family, which also produced *Ebony* and *Jet* magazines. The vibrant cover features a young Michael Jackson, who at the time was a global sensation as the lead singer of The Jackson 5. Smiling warmly, Michael holds a globe in his left hand, symbolizing his emerging international stardom and the group's extensive world travels.

    The cover teases articles and features such as "Olympic Hopefuls," "Yankee Doodle Disco," and "Summer Games & Stories," reflecting the magazine's mission to educate and entertain African American youth with culturally relevant and inspiring content.

    Michael Jackson's appearance on the cover underscores his influence as a role model for children and his connection to themes of empowerment, creativity, and global impact. This issue is a treasured artifact of both Jackson's early career and the legacy of *Ebony Jr!* in providing representation and inspiration for young Black audiences during the 1970s.

JACKSON 5 ALPHABITS CEREAL PROMO RECORD (1970s): BLENDING MUSIC AND CONSUMER CULTURE.

The Jackson Five were featured on this vintage promotional record created as a giveaway for Alpha-Bits cereal in the 1970s. The colorful, circular design mimics a vinyl record, showcasing a vibrant image of the iconic Motown group—Michael, Jermaine, Jackie, Tito, and Marlon Jackson. The record prominently features the Motown logo and the title "Jackson Five," alongside a tracklist of their classic hits, including "ABC," "I Want You Back," "I'll Bet You," "Darling Dear," and "Maybe Tomorrow."

This promotional item was part of a marketing campaign that blended the cultural popularity of The Jackson Five with breakfast cereal, targeting families and children during the group's meteoric rise to fame. As one of the most successful acts of the Motown era, The Jackson Five's youthful energy and wide appeal made them a perfect fit for this type of cross-promotional product.

Artifacts like this capture the intersection of music and consumer culture during the 1970s, illustrating how companies leveraged the star power of Black artists to market products to a broad audience. Today, this item serves as both a nostalgic collectible and a reminder of the group's immense impact on popular culture.

Compulsive Magazine Cover Featuring MC Sha-Rock: A Hip-Hop Luminary

This *Compulsive* magazine cover celebrates MC Sha-Rock, an iconic figure and trailblazer in hip-hop culture, prominently billed as the "First Female MC of Hip-Hop Culture." The cover captures her commanding presence and highlights her immense contribution to the genre, solidifying her legacy as a luminary in the male-dominated early days of hip-hop.

MC Sha-Rock, born Sharon Green, rose to prominence in the late 1970s as a member of the Funky 4 + 1, the first hip-hop group to feature a female MC. The group made history in 1981 as the first hip-hop act to perform on national television, appearing on *Saturday Night Live*. Her pioneering style and commanding delivery paved the way for women in hip-hop, breaking barriers and setting the standard for future female MCs.

As an enduring cultural figure, MC Sha-Rock's contributions are celebrated for laying the foundation for gender inclusivity in hip-hop and for shaping its evolution as a global art form. Her legacy continues to inspire new generations of artists, emphasizing the transformative power of representation and resilience in music.

This magazine cover not only honors MC Sha-Rock's groundbreaking achievements but also underscores the cultural importance of recognizing the women who have shaped hip-hop history from its earliest days. Sha Rock signed this cover when she was a guest speaker with the Black History 101 Mobile Museum at the University of Wyoming.

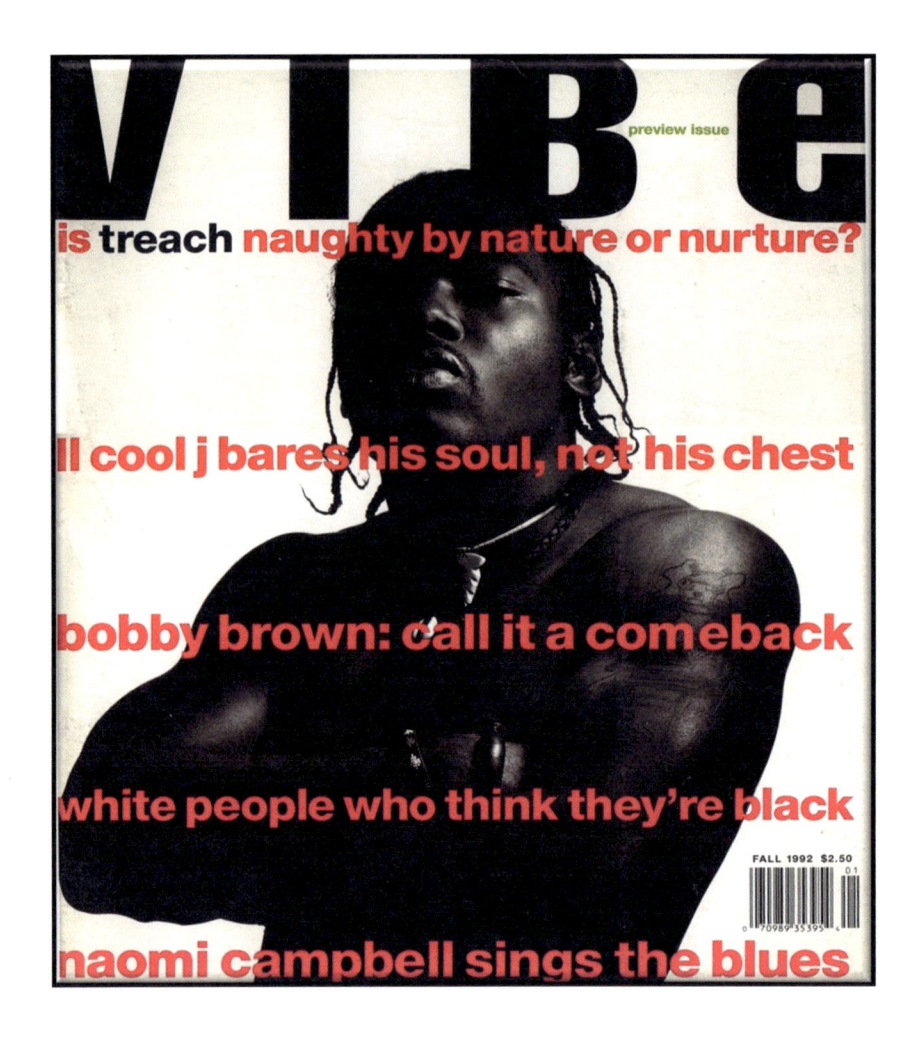

**VIBE Magazine Premiere Cover with Treach (1992):
Celebrating the intersection of hip-hop and media.**

The premiere issue of *VIBE* magazine, released in Fall 1992, featuring Treach of Naughty by Nature on its cover. Treach, a prominent figure in hip-hop during the early '90s, is captured in a powerful pose that highlights his commanding presence and charisma, symbolizing his role as a voice for the streets and a leader in the burgeoning era of mainstream rap.

The issue explores themes of music, culture, and identity. This inaugural issue set the tone for *VIBE* magazine as a trailblazing publication that would blend music, culture, fashion, and social commentary. Founded by Quincy Jones, *VIBE* became a cornerstone in documenting the hip-hop and R&B movements, as well as the broader cultural shifts of the '90s and beyond. Treach's presence on the first cover underscores the magazine's commitment to showcasing authentic voices and influential figures shaping urban culture.

J DILLA ON REAL DETROIT MAGAZINE (2006): HONORING HIS TRANSFORMATIVE IMPACT ON HIP-HOP PRODUCTION.

This is a February 2006 edition of *Real Detroit Weekly* featuring a tribute to James "J Dilla" Yancey (1974–2006) on its cover. The striking illustration of J Dilla, adorned with his signature chain and cap, highlights his profound influence on hip-hop and music production. Known as one of Detroit's greatest musical innovators, J Dilla revolutionized the soundscape of hip-hop with his soulful and intricate beats, collaborating with iconic artists and groups such as A Tribe Called Quest, Common, and Slum Village. This issue honors his legacy shortly after his untimely passing, capturing the city's deep admiration for his artistry and celebrating his indelible impact on global music culture.

CHAPTER 4

THE ABSURDITY OF WHITENESS: CONFRONTING EVERYDAY RACISM

As I examine the artifacts in this section, I am struck by how racism was present in the very fabric of daily life—through objects that may seem trivial or nostalgic on the surface but carry deeply harmful messages. These artifacts expose what I call *white absurdity*—a framework for understanding the irrational yet deliberate ways that whiteness has positioned itself as the standard while marginalizing others. By normalizing this absurdity, society has created a space where everyday people can perpetuate harmful ideas without recognizing their complicity.

I avoid using the term "white supremacy" to describe this dynamic because the language itself is flawed. The word "supremacy" falsely elevates whiteness, giving it an unearned sense of superiority. Worse, it creates a convenient psychological distance for people who don't see themselves as "white supremacists" or aligned with groups like the KKK or Nazis. This disconnect allows many to view racism as something extreme, confined to the margins of society, rather than recognizing it as a pervasive and systemic issue that operates in subtle and insidious ways.

The artifacts featured here reveal how the normalization of whiteness historically has shaped culture in ways that are absurd and dangerous. A lynching photograph from Marion, Indiana (1930), turned into a macabre souvenir, captures the everyday acceptance of racial violence. Toys like the Topsy-Turvy doll or games like the Sambo Target Game disguise dehumanization as play, embedding harmful ideas in children's minds. Even household items like a Mammy grocery list or a Valentine's card with racist puns trivialize and perpetuate harmful stereotypes, making them part of the mundane.

What's more, these seemingly absurd objects weren't just tools of cultural indoctrination; they were used as justifications for laws and policies that restricted Black people's social mobility for decades. The dehumanizing caricatures portrayed in items like these were often cited in political discourse as evidence of Black inferiority, rationalizing segregation, disenfranchisement, and discriminatory practices in housing, education, and employment. By embedding racism in the everyday, these objects helped sustain the legal and economic frameworks that kept Black people oppressed under the guise of maintaining "order" or "tradition."

These objects may seem ridiculous—laughable even—but that is precisely the point. The absurdity lies in how such blatant racism was presented as normal, even charming. The very act of dismissing these objects as products of the past or relics of a "different time" further perpetuates this absurdity by refusing to confront the harm they caused and continue to cause.

Through this collection, I invite readers to confront the absurdity of whiteness—not as an indictment of individual people, but as a way to understand how systems of power operate in seemingly mundane ways. By recognizing the absurdity of these artifacts and their impact, we can begin the difficult but necessary work of dismantling the structures and beliefs that uphold racism.

WHITE ABSURDITY FRAMEWORK

1. "Whiteness" is a social construct based on the false notion of racial "supremacy" and the dehumanization of people of color.
Example: *The legal classification of African Americans as "three-fifths of a person" in the U.S. Constitution during the 18th century exemplifies the creation of a racial hierarchy that dehumanized Black people for the benefit of maintaining white supremacy in the political system.*

2. A set of pathological ideas and behaviors created in the "white" imagination that has real life consequences for people of color.
Example: *The stereotype of Black criminality, perpetuated through media and public policy, has led to the disproportionate incarceration of Black individuals under laws like the 1994 Crime Bill, resulting in systemic barriers for generations.*

3. Manifests itself in subtle and overt ways.
Example: *Subtly, this is reflected in workplace discrimination where resumes with "ethnic-sounding" names receive fewer callbacks compared to identical resumes with "white-sounding" names. Overtly, it's visible in acts of police brutality like the murder of George Floyd.*

4. Created a society of unjust laws, policies, and social norms privileging whites by giving an unfair economic advantage over people of color.
Example: *Redlining practices in the 20th century prevented Black families from buying homes in certain neighborhoods, restricting their access to generational wealth while allowing white families to build financial stability.*

5. Makes excuses for the inexcusable.
Example: *The defense of Confederate monuments as "heritage" rather than symbols of racial oppression ignores the fact that these monuments were erected during the Jim Crow era to intimidate Black communities and uphold white supremacy.*

6. Obstructs the progress of marginalized people and society as a whole.
Example: *The defunding of affirmative action programs limits educational and professional opportunities for people of color, reinforcing systemic inequality while depriving society of the benefits of diverse perspectives and contributions.*

7. Is situated in a narrative that justifies the actions of "white" people regardless of the absurdity, inhumanity, or lack of factual support.
Example: *The narrative that European colonization of Indigenous lands was part of a "civilizing mission" ignores the genocide and displacement of Indigenous peoples, justifying these actions under the guise of progress and manifest destiny.*

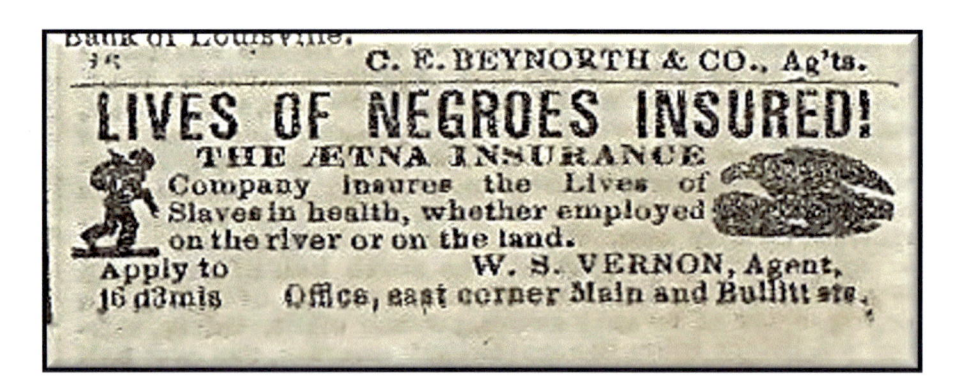

"LIVES OF NEGROES INSURED!": THE COMMODIFICATION OF BLACK BODIES

This historical classified advertisement for Aetna Insurance Company, titled "Lives of Negroes Insured!", starkly illustrates the dehumanization and commodification of Black bodies during the era of slavery. The ad promotes life insurance policies for enslaved people, treating them not as human beings but as property to protect the economic interests of enslavers. These policies allowed enslavers to recover financial losses in the event of an enslaved person's death, reducing human life to a mere economic asset.

Such practices were not isolated but part of a broader system in which major institutions and industries directly profited from slavery. Insurance companies like Aetna, banks such as JP Morgan Chase and Wells Fargo, and others like New York Life Insurance issued policies on enslaved individuals, accepted enslaved people as collateral for loans, or supported industries reliant on enslaved labor. These actions intertwined the institution of slavery with the growth of American financial systems, creating wealth that still impacts the economic landscape today.

The legacy of these practices is deeply felt in the persistent racial wealth gap and systemic inequities that continue to disadvantage African Americans. This advertisement serves as a stark reminder of how integral slavery was to the development of American capitalism and how institutions that profited from this brutal system have yet to fully reckon with their role in perpetuating racial injustice.

In recent years, some corporations have acknowledged their historical ties to slavery, with varying degrees of accountability. Efforts have included issuing apologies, funding research into their histories, and supporting racial equity initiatives. However, this ad underscores the need for a broader, more systemic approach to addressing the enduring economic and social effects of slavery—an acknowledgment of history tied to a commitment to reparative action.

SCENES IN MEMPHIS, TENNESSEE, DURING THE RIOT—BURNING A FREEDMEN'S SCHOOL-HOUSE.
[Sketched by A. R. W.]

THE MEMPHIS MASSACRE OF 1866: BURNING OF A FREEDMEN'S SCHOOL AND THE LEGACY OF WHITE SUPREMACY.

In May 1866, Memphis, Tennessee, became the site of the Memphis Massacre, a violent racial attack targeting African Americans. Over three days, white mobs, including police and firemen, killed at least 46 Black residents, destroyed homes, churches, and businesses, and burned freedmen's schools to the ground. These schools, symbols of hope and empowerment for formerly enslaved individuals, were intentionally targeted to suppress Black education and social progress.

The event, captured in a striking illustration titled "Scenes in Memphis, Tennessee, During the Riot—Burning a Freedmen's School-House," appeared in the May 26, 1866, edition of *Harper's Weekly*. Sketched by Alfred R. Waud, the image graphically depicts the mob's violent efforts to destroy one of these schools, emphasizing the deep racial animosity and systemic oppression faced by African Americans during Reconstruction.

This act reflects the concept of white absurdity—the irrational and violent measures white supremacists employed to maintain racial dominance, even when it undermined societal progress. The destruction of institutions like freedmen's schools not only stunted the potential for collective growth but also revealed the absurd fear of Black empowerment that fueled such actions. This tragic event stands as a stark reminder of the lengths to which white supremacy has gone to resist equality, making it a pivotal moment in the struggle for civil rights in America.

THE LYNCHING OF THOMAS SHIPP AND ABRAM SMITH IN MARION, INDIANA (1930): A SYMBOL OF RACIAL TERROR

The photograph from Marion, Indiana, depicting the lynching of Thomas Shipp and Abram Smith on August 7, 1930, is a haunting and brutal reminder of racial violence in America. The two young Black men were accused of a crime without trial, dragged from their jail cells by a white mob, and hanged in front of a large crowd. This act of extrajudicial terror was witnessed by onlookers who posed for the photograph, some even smiling, highlighting the normalized brutality of such events in Jim Crow-era America.

A third man, James Cameron, survived the lynching after the mob inexplicably spared him. Cameron later became a prominent voice against racial violence and founded America's Black Holocaust Museum in Milwaukee, Wisconsin, to preserve the memory of victims of lynching and to educate future generations about the horrors of racial injustice.

The image's legacy extends into art and activism. It inspired Abel Meeropol's poem "Strange Fruit," famously performed by Billie Holiday, which became one of the most haunting songs of the 20th century, condemning the atrocities of lynching. Decades later, the photograph was used by Public Enemy as the cover for their single "Hazy Shade of Criminal," tying the historic violence of lynching to ongoing systemic racism in America.

Big Meeting
KU KLUX KLAN
Tuesday Night!

Patriotic Lecture:

"Why the Knights of the Ku Klux Klan"

By EVANGELIST HOMER KELLEMS

Enthusiastic Community Singing

Led by Evangelist Cecil Brooks.

Beautiful Special Musical Numbers

By the Kellems-Brooks Company
Nationally Known Evangelists

Bring the whole family to hear them in this big Outdoor Service.

At the Lighted Cross, South End of C Street

VICTORVILLE

SILVER OFFERING   8:00 o'clock

KKK Meeting Flyer, Robe, and Business Card: Propaganda of the absurd.

    These three Ku Klux Klan artifacts—a Victorville meeting flyer, a business card declaring "Klan Country," and an ornate robe with hood and crimson sash—reflect the calculated efforts of the Klan to normalize their ideology and embed themselves in American society. The flyer and business card use community-friendly language and imagery to mask the Klan's agenda of hate, inviting families to participate in events or associate with their organization under the guise of patriotism and moral order. The robe, with its ceremonial design and symbols, exemplifies how the Klan elevated their ideology with the illusion of tradition and authority, projecting power while maintaining anonymity.

    Together, these artifacts illustrate the absurdity of whiteness, a concept that highlights how racism and exclusion were framed as righteous and even institutionalized through community events, professional branding, and symbolic regalia. They reveal how the Klan attempted to make their hateful ideology appear acceptable, blending intimidation and propaganda to sustain systemic oppression while fostering disconnection between their actions and the public's perception of racism. These artifacts serve as stark reminders of how organizations like the Klan sought to legitimize their agenda and perpetuate fear in everyday life.

1933 Poll Tax Receipt: A Symbol of Racial Inequality in Voting Rights

The poll tax receipt from Travis County, Texas, issued in 1933, is a tangible artifact of a systemic barrier used to restrict voting access. Poll taxes, implemented in many Southern states after Reconstruction, required individuals to pay a fee to register to vote, disproportionately disenfranchising African Americans, poor whites, and other marginalized groups.

For many white citizens, paying the poll tax was a financial inconvenience, but it did not deny their access to the democratic process. Conversely, for African Americans, the tax was often an insurmountable barrier. Coupled with literacy tests, intimidation, and violence, poll taxes effectively excluded millions of Black citizens from voting, ensuring white supremacy in political systems.

It wasn't until the 24th Amendment in 1964 and the Voting Rights Act of 1965 that poll taxes were abolished at the federal level. This receipt serves as a reminder of the enduring struggle for voting rights and the ongoing efforts to combat voter suppression in various forms.

SERVED WITH A SIDE OF STEREOTYPES: COON CHICKEN INN PLATE

This plate, featuring the caricatured logo of the "Coon Chicken Inn," represents a period in American history when racial stereotypes were frequently used in advertising and branding. The imagery, which includes exaggerated features, was central to the restaurant chain's marketing, reflecting the normalized racism of the early to mid-20th century. The Coon Chicken Inn, founded in the 1920s, used this offensive depiction as its mascot and branding strategy, embedding such imagery into everyday items like this plate.

Today, artifacts like this are preserved as educational tools, highlighting the ways systemic racism influenced cultural and commercial practices. They serve as critical resources for understanding and addressing the legacy of racial stereotyping in American history.

JIM CROW ERA SEGREGATION SIGN: A SEPARATE AND UNEQUAL PAST.

The Montgomery segregation sign, which directed "White" and "Colored" individuals to separate drinking fountains, stands as a stark embodiment of the absurdity and cruelty of white supremacy. It lays bare the irrational extremes to which society went to enforce fabricated racial distinctions, codifying these biases into the everyday lives of millions. The segregation of something as fundamental and universal as water underscores the pettiness and insecurity of a system built on the illusion of racial hierarchy. By institutionalizing such dehumanizing practices, white supremacy attempted to assert dominance in even the most mundane aspects of existence, reinforcing the false notion of superiority by denying African Americans access to equal facilities and rights.

This sign is not just a relic of the Jim Crow era but a potent artifact that symbolizes the deep roots of systemic racism in America. It serves as a tangible reminder of the lengths to which power structures went to preserve inequality, using public spaces as a stage to propagate exclusion and humiliation. The weathered and rusted condition of the sign today contrasts sharply with the enduring legacies of systemic racism it represents, reminding us that while the physical markers of segregation may fade, their societal impacts persist.

Ultimately, this sign challenges us to critically reflect on the absurdity and senselessness of institutionalized racism. It forces us to confront uncomfortable truths about a past that is not as distant as we might hope and compels us to address the ways in which these legacies continue to shape our present. It is a call to action—demanding that we acknowledge the enduring harm of such practices and actively work to dismantle the remnants of these systems in pursuit of justice and equality.

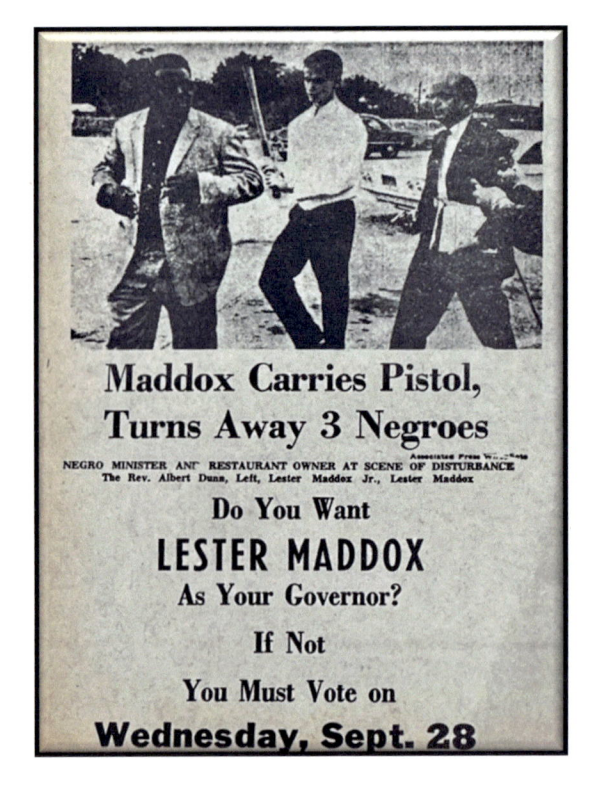

ANTI-LESTER MADDOX FLYER AND AX HANDLE: DOCUMENTING RESISTANCE TO DESEGREGATION.

  The flyer, "Maddox Carries Pistol, Turns Away 3 Negroes," and the signed "Pickrick Drumstick" encapsulate the violent and deeply divisive ideology of Lester Maddox during the civil rights era. The flyer highlights Maddox's use of a pistol and bat to intimidate Black patrons at his restaurant, framing his hostility as a campaign issue for voters to consider. Meanwhile, the signed ax handle showcases how Maddox commodified his segregationist stance, turning a tool of violence into a promotional item to celebrate his opposition to integration.

  Together, these artifacts demonstrate what I describe as *white absurdity*: the deliberate yet illogical framing of racist actions as symbols of strength, leadership, and even pride. Maddox's ability to weaponize these acts of aggression, not only in practice but as a means of gaining political traction, illustrates the absurd ways in which whiteness was upheld and normalized. These objects challenge us to confront the moral contradictions of this era and the systems that allowed such figures to thrive.

ANTI-"NEGRO RECORDS" FLYER:
EXPOSING RACISM IN MUSIC INDUSTRY OPPOSITION

The Citizens' Council of Greater New Orleans, Inc., issued this flyer in 1960 aimed at discouraging the purchase and consumption of music by Black artists. Boldly titled *"NOTICE! STOP"*, the flyer urges white Americans to *"Help Save The Youth of America"* by boycotting what it derogatorily refers to as *"Negro Records."*

The flyer claims that the music created by Black artists, characterized as *"screaming, idiotic words, and savage music,"* is undermining the morals of white youth. It appeals to business owners by stating, *"If you don't want to serve negroes in your place of business, then do not have negro records on your juke box or listen to negro records on the radio."*

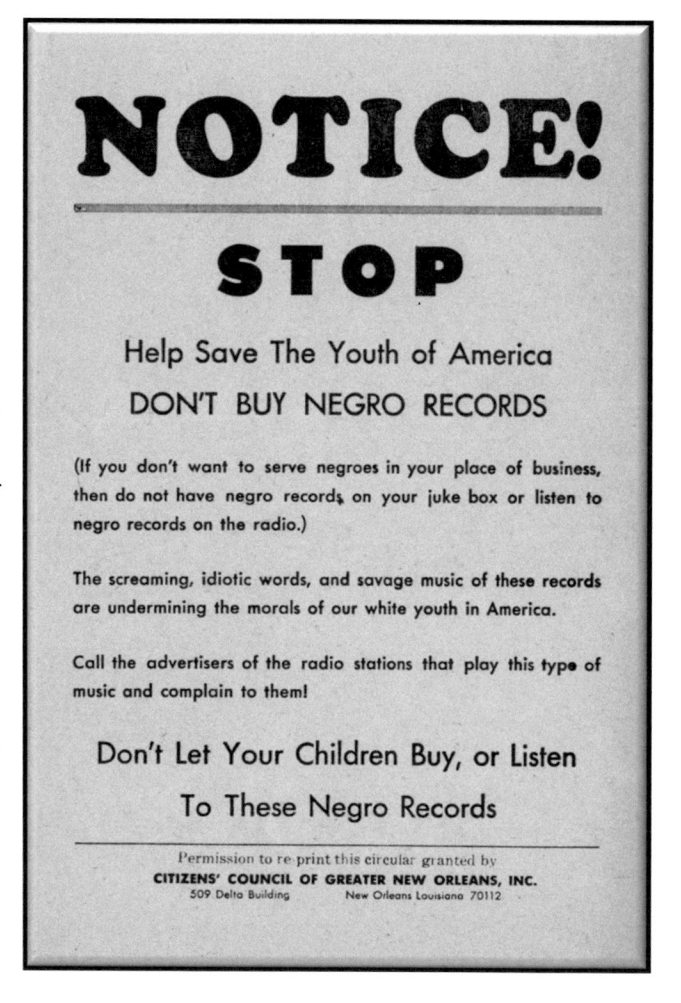

The document also encourages readers to call advertisers of radio stations that play such music and to complain, to stifle the growing influence of Black culture and its contribution to music genres like rock 'n' roll, jazz, and R&B, which were gaining widespread popularity at the time.

The flyer concludes with a warning to parents, *"Don't Let Your Children Buy, or Listen To These Negro Records,"* reinforcing the segregationist and white supremacist ideologies of the Citizens' Council, a group known for its opposition to racial integration and civil rights.

This flyer is a reflects the lengths to which segregationist organizations went to stifle Black cultural expression, using fear and propaganda to maintain racial division and suppress the transformative power of music in breaking down social barriers. Today, it serves as a undeniable evidence of systemic racism and the cultural resistance faced by Black artists during this era.

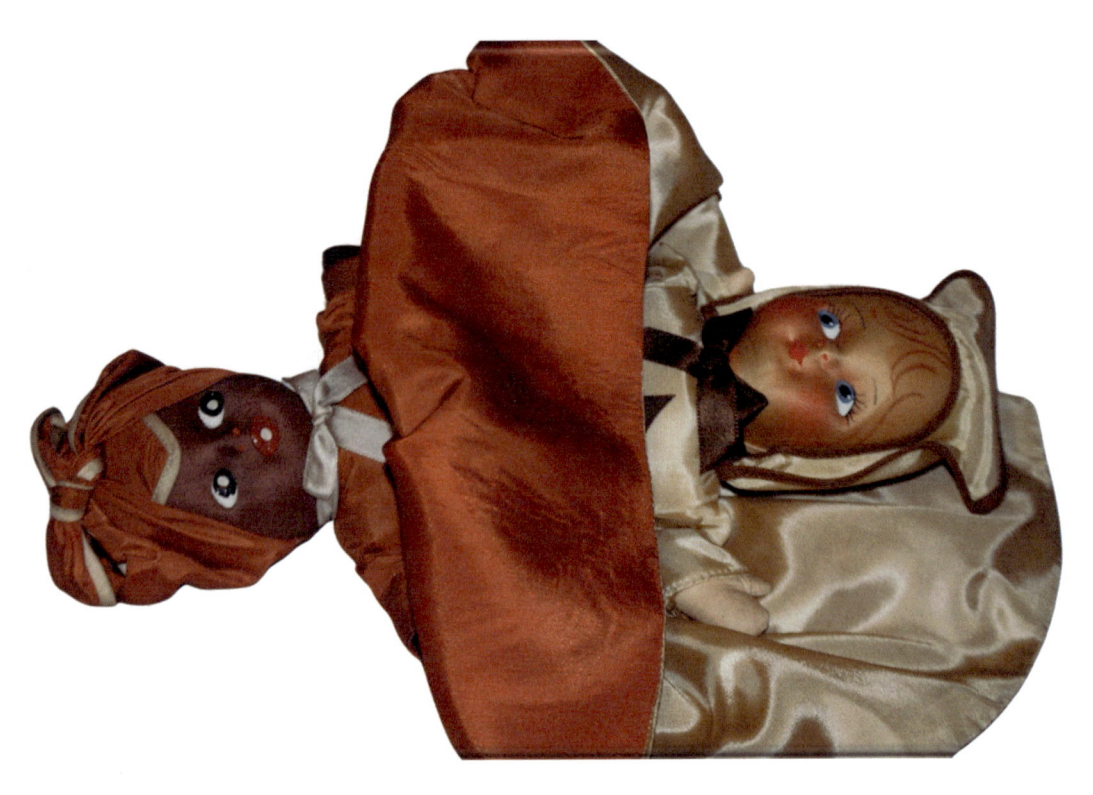

TOPSY-TURVY DOLL: RACISM AS CHILD'S PLAY.

The Topsy-Turvy doll, a reversible toy with a white doll on one side and a Black doll on the other, reflects the deeply ingrained racial hierarchies of American society during the Civil War era. Given to white children, these dolls served as tools of indoctrination, encouraging children to role-play as "masters" over "slaves" and reinforcing ideas of white dominance at an impressionable age. The white doll, dressed in elegant clothing, symbolized privilege and beauty, while the Black doll, in simpler attire, embodied subservience and marginalization, perpetuating harmful stereotypes.

This artifact exemplifies *white absurdity*, the deliberate yet illogical normalization of whiteness as superior, even in childhood toys. By embedding racial hierarchies into play, society disguised systemic racism as harmless entertainment, teaching children to accept and perpetuate inequality as natural. The doll's symbolism aligns with the findings of the 1950 Clark Doll Experiment and its later recreation in Kiri Davis's 2005 film, both of which revealed the damaging effects of racial bias on children's self-perception, underscoring the persistence of systemic racism.

As an artifact, the Topsy-Turvy doll reveals the absurdity of framing oppressive systems as benign traditions. It forces us to confront how everyday objects, even toys, have been used to sustain racial inequality and the lasting psychological impact of such practices.

Topsy-Turvy Easter Bunny Toy: Embodying racial hierarchies in toys.

Topsy Turvy and the Easter Bunny is a vintage children's book whose imagery and narrative reflect the racial biases and stereotypes of its time. The cover features Topsy Turvy, a caricatured Black doll-like figure with exaggerated features, riding a donkey alongside a cartoonish Easter Bunny. Rendered in a minstrel-inspired style and dressed in brightly colored clothing, Topsy Turvy embodies harmful stereotypes that were normalized in mid-20th-century children's literature.

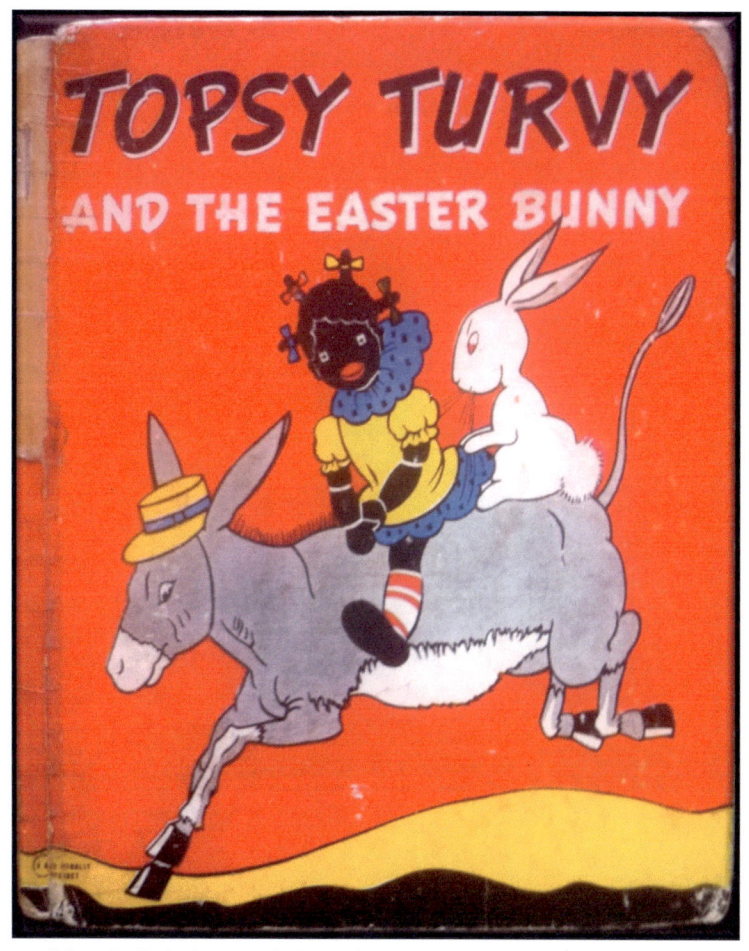

The book's attempt to blend lighthearted holiday themes with dehumanizing depictions of Black characters highlights the problematic intent of such works. By marketing books like this to children, publishers not only reinforced racist imagery but also embedded discriminatory attitudes into the cultural consciousness at a young age. Stories like these perpetuated white dominance and positioned Blackness as inferior, framing systemic racism as innocent entertainment.

This artifact exemplifies *white absurdity*—the calculated yet irrational process by which whiteness is framed as superior while dehumanizing others is disguised as tradition or humor. By embedding racism in children's stories, society normalized oppressive ideas and absolved readers of their harmful implications. Topsy Turvy and the Easter Bunny is a troubling reminder of how cultural materials were used to perpetuate bias and indoctrinate future generations, making it a critical artifact for examining the enduring legacy of systemic racism in popular culture.

THE ADVENTURES OF LITTLE BLACK SAMBO BOARD GAME: A REFLECTION OF RACIAL STEREOTYPES IN POPULAR CULTURE

The Adventures of Little Black Sambo, was released in the early-to-mid 20th century, a time when deeply ingrained racial stereotypes permeated popular media and entertainment. Based on the controversial 1899 book by Helen Bannerman, the game draws heavily from the caricatured imagery of the original story, depicting its characters with exaggerated and offensive features that perpetuate harmful racial stereotypes.

The game's premise follows the titular character as he encounters tigers, loses his clothing, and ultimately retrieves them, mirroring the book's storyline. The colorful design and whimsical portrayal of events mask the insidious stereotypes embedded in its imagery, which were normalized in its time. This game, like the book, gained significant popularity among white audiences in the U.S. and Europe, where such imagery was both consumed and perpetuated as entertainment.

However, as civil rights movements gained momentum, both the book and its derivative products, including this board game, faced increasing pushback. Critics condemned the overtly racist depictions and the reductive portrayal of Black characters as absurd and dehumanizing. By the late 20th century, the game, along with other merchandise tied to the story, had become emblematic of the systemic racism embedded in popular culture.

The absurdity of such a game lies in its ability to trivialize serious issues of racial stereotyping and discrimination, reducing them to a child's game,

Nigger Hair Tobacco: A Disturbing Reflection of Racism in Consumer Culture.

  The Nigger Hair Tobacco brand, sold in the late 19th and early 20th centuries, represents one of the most overt and dehumanizing examples of racism in American consumer culture. Its packaging featured a grotesque caricature of a Black person with exaggerated features, designed to capitalize on and reinforce racist stereotypes for commercial gain. The name and imagery epitomize how racism was not only socially accepted but commodified, embedding white dominance into everyday transactions.

  Metaphorically, the act of burning this tobacco carries a chilling form of symbolic violence. As consumers lit their pipes or cigars, they participated—knowingly or not—in an act of racial erasure, turning the dehumanized image of Blackness into ash. This act extends beyond literal consumption, representing how systems of oppression consumed and destroyed Black dignity for the benefit of white consumer culture.

  Today, this artifact serves as a stark reminder of how deeply embedded racism was—and in many ways still is—in everyday life. It underscores the need to confront the lingering legacy of racial exploitation and to dismantle the systems that continue to perpetuate inequality. By studying such artifacts, we can expose the absurdity of these normalized injustices and ensure they are neither repeated nor forgotten.

Ogden's Cigarettes "Group of Nigger Boys" Cards: Offensive marketing materials.

Ogden's Cigarettes trade cards featured a photograph titled "Group of N***** Boys," reflecting the deeply ingrained racial stereotypes and systemic racism in advertising during the late 19th and early 20th centuries. Cigarette trade cards, popular as collectible items, were used as promotional tools and often perpetuated the biases of their time. This card dehumanizes its subjects, reducing Black individuals to caricatures designed to entertain and appeal to a white consumer base.

Ogden's Tobacco Company, established in Liverpool in 1860, became a leading player in the global tobacco industry and a major producer of cigarette cards. These cards, which depicted themes ranging from sports to landscapes, also included racist imagery that commodified marginalized groups. By the early 20th century, Ogden's became part of the Imperial Tobacco Company, embedding its legacy within a larger corporate framework.

The card is a sobering reminder of how racism was embedded in seemingly mundane aspects of life, reinforcing social hierarchies through commerce. It challenges us to recognize the calculated normalization of these absurd narratives and to confront their lingering impact on societal perceptions and racial inequality.

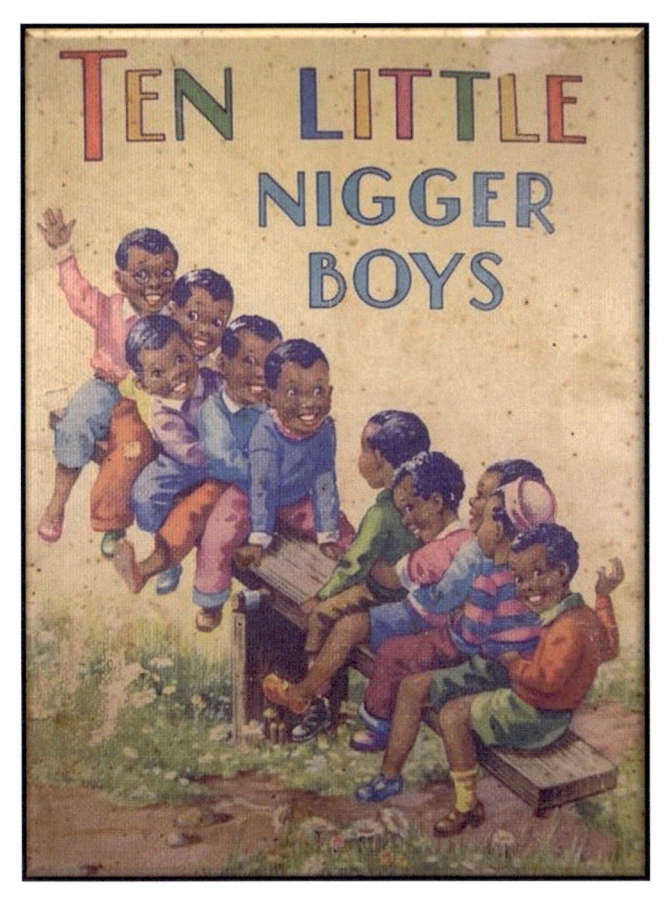

TEN LITTLE NIGGER BOYS BOOK: A CHILDREN'S BOOK PROMOTING HARMFUL STEREOTYPES.

The book *Ten Little N**r Boys* is an unsettling example of racist children's literature widely published in the late 19th and early 20th centuries. Its title and content reflect the pervasive normalization of racial stereotypes and dehumanizing depictions of Black people in popular culture during that time. Structured as a nursery rhyme, the story follows ten caricatured Black children who, through a series of violent and absurd events, are reduced to none, ending with the chilling phrase, "and then there were none." This grim refrain also served as the title for an Agatha Christie novel, further embedding this narrative structure into broader cultural consciousness.

The cover features exaggerated and cartoonish depictions of Black children, a visual style commonly used in media and literature to ridicule and diminish African Americans. Books like this, marketed as lighthearted entertainment for white audiences, perpetuated harmful ideas that upheld systemic racism and reinforced racial hierarchies through humor and storytelling. The structure and theme of the book make it, metaphorically, a nursery rhyme of genocide, framing the systematic erasure of Black lives as acceptable and even entertaining.

A modern adaptation of this format persists in *Ten Little Monkeys*, which replaces human figures with animals. While no longer explicitly tied to racist imagery, the continued use of the format obscures the violent and dehumanizing origins of such stories, allowing their legacy to persist without scrutiny.

This book underscores how racism was deeply embedded in children's education and entertainment, shaping perceptions and normalizing prejudice for generations. While offensive and painful, it serves as a critical tool for understanding the cultural mechanisms that sustained systemic racism and offers an opportunity to confront and dismantle these harmful narratives in contemporary society.

Sambo Target Game (1920s): A grotesque game reflecting systemic racism.

The Sambo Target Game was manufactured in the 1920s by the All Metals Company in Wyandotte, Michigan. The game features a highly offensive caricature of a Black boy, "Sambo," with exaggerated facial features, including a wide grin, bulging eyes, and bright red lips. The boy is depicted in colorful, stereotypical clothing, placed in front of a target with point values ranging from 100 to 1,000. The vibrant design also includes cartoonish tropical elements such as a bird and palm trees.

The game's premise is as blatant as it is disturbing: Blackness itself is literally the target. Children would throw objects at the metal board, aiming at the bullseye set on the character's body. This "game" exemplifies how racism was embedded into everyday entertainment, indoctrinating children with dehumanizing stereotypes and reinforcing systemic oppression under the guise of play.

Being the target of racism is nothing new. This artifact starkly demonstrates how racism was not only normalized but commercialized. Through games like this, Black children and adults were reduced to objects of ridicule, perpetuating harmful narratives that have long-lasting psychological and social implications.

This Sambo Target Game is a clear reminder of how racist ideologies infiltrated all aspects of life, from advertising to childhood recreation, in the early 20th century. Today, it serves as an important but unsettling artifact, prompting critical discussions about the pervasive and systemic nature of racism in American history.

LAUTZ BROS. SOAP ADVERTISEMENT: DEHUMANIZING DEPICTIONS OF BLACKNESS.

Lautz Bros. & Co. Soaps designed this troubling trade card reflecting the pervasive racism in marketing and advertising during the late 19th and early 20th centuries. The illustration depicts a white man, ostensibly an authority figure, scrubbing a Black man's skin with soap in an exaggerated and dehumanizing manner. The Black man's features are distorted into racist caricature, a common visual trope used to mock and belittle African Americans during this period.

The advertisement not only promotes the soap but also uses the concept of "cleansing" as a metaphor to perpetuate racist ideologies, suggesting that Blackness itself is something to be "washed away." This imagery reflects the deeply entrenched stereotypes of the era, where Black individuals were often depicted in servile or inferior roles, reinforcing notions of white superiority.

Products like Lautz Bros. Soap used these racist depictions as a means to appeal to white consumers, embedding racism into everyday commercial practices. Today, advertisements like this reflect the ways racism was normalized and commodified in American society. They are critical artifacts for understanding the intersection of commerce, media, and systemic racism, emphasizing the importance of confronting and acknowledging these painful chapters in history.

Mammy Grocery List: Reinforcing Stereotypes in Everyday Items.

This grocery list, featuring a stereotypical "Mammy" figure with exaggerated features and the caption "Reckon Ah Needs?" illustrates how *white absurdity* was embedded in everyday life. The Mammy archetype, a romanticized caricature of the Antebellum South, portrayed Black women as devoted domestic servants, perpetuating the absurd notion that they were content in subservience to white households. This idealized image served to mask the harsh realities of systemic oppression and exploitation.

Items like this, marketed to white consumers, combined functionality with racist imagery, seamlessly integrating dehumanizing stereotypes into daily routines. This absurd normalization trivialized the lived experiences of Black women and justified racial hierarchies by framing servitude as natural and even endearing. The presence of such imagery in mundane objects like a grocery list highlights how racism was perpetuated not only through overt violence but also through subtle reinforcements in everyday culture.

Today, artifacts like this compel us to confront the absurdity of a society that embedded and celebrated such stereotypes in the ordinary, challenging us to examine how these narratives continue to influence cultural perceptions and systemic inequality. They reveal the calculated ways whiteness positioned itself as superior while disguising oppression as harmless tradition.

"I AIN'T PICKIN-ANY BODY BUT YOU" VALENTINE'S DAY CARD: A RACIST TAKE ON ROMANTIC HUMOR.

The card, titled *"I Ain't Pickin-Any Body But You, Valentine,"* features a caricature of a young Black girl depicted as a stereotypical "pickaninny," a deeply offensive and outdated trope. The illustration portrays the girl with exaggerated facial features, a tattered dress, and unkempt hair tied with bows, standing barefoot in a rural setting. She holds a heart-shaped sign bearing the card's message, which plays on a pun using the racial slur. This card reflects the racial insensitivity and prejudice prevalent in American popular culture during the early 20th century.

112

GOLLIWOG DOLL: A TOY POPULARIZING RACIST CARICATURES.

This doll is a modern representation of a Golliwog, a caricature originally introduced in the late 19th century and widely used throughout the 20th century. The Golliwog character first appeared in Florence Kate Upton's 1895 children's book *The Adventures of Two Dutch Dolls and a Golliwogg*, where it was described as "a horrid sight" but portrayed as a friendly companion. Despite its innocent introduction, the Golliwog quickly became a symbol of racial stereotypes, often associated with exaggerated physical features and negative connotations about Black people.

The doll shown here wears the classic Golliwog attire: brightly colored clothing, including a blue jacket, yellow vest, red and white striped trousers, and a red bow tie. Its wide eyes, exaggerated red lips, and frizzy black hair are hallmarks of the caricature.

Over time, Golliwogs became a popular image in marketing and collectibles, appearing on toys, books, and even advertisements. However, as cultural awareness grew, the Golliwog came to symbolize racism and prejudice, and its continued production and sale have been the subject of widespread criticism. While some view it as a nostalgic item, many see it as a painful reminder of systemic racism and the dehumanization of Black people.

DELAWARE WHIPPING POST, DOVER, DEL.

Delaware Whipping Post Postcard:
Reflecting systemic violence.

Whipping posts were used as a method of corporal punishment in the United States, with Delaware being one of the last states to officially abolish their use in 1972. This captures a public whipping, showing a Black man tied to the post as an executioner prepares to administer lashes while a crowd, including children, gathers to watch.

The scene reflects a brutal era when corporal punishment was not only legal but also a spectacle. The whipping post in Delaware was primarily used for punishing petty crimes, often disproportionately targeting African Americans, both during slavery and after its abolition. This public humiliation served as a means of enforcing racial hierarchy and social control, perpetuating the dehumanization of Black individuals.

This postcard serves as a reminder of the systemic violence inflicted on African Americans and the normalization of cruelty in American society. The presence of onlookers, including children, highlights the cultural desensitization to such practices.

Chapter 5

BEYOND BORDERS: GLOBAL BLACK INFLUENCE

The reach of Black creativity and activism knows no boundaries, transcending geographic, cultural, and linguistic barriers to leave an indelible mark on the world. This section, Beyond Borders: Global Black Influence, examines how Black artists, thinkers, and movements have not only shaped their local communities but also inspired global dialogues on identity, freedom, and culture. The artifacts presented here reflect a powerful narrative of connection and exchange, showcasing the international resonance of Black excellence, resistance, and innovation.

From the intellectual vibrancy of the Pan-African movement to the global expansion of hip-hop and the universal appeal of cultural icons like Muhammad Ali, these artifacts tell a story of how Black expression has united people across continents. The Poster for the Second Conference of Negro Writers and Artists, for example, highlights the efforts of luminaries such as Aimé Césaire and Frantz Fanon to foster Pan-African dialogue on art and identity in a decolonizing world. As Léopold Sédar Senghor famously stated, "Art is the soul of a people. It expresses their innermost identity and their vision of the world." This poster captures the essence of how culture became a rallying point for solidarity and resistance.

Other pieces reflect the extraordinary valor and influence of individuals and movements. The Harlem Hellfighters photo for instance, honors the bravery of the 369th Infantry Regiment during World War I, whose military achievements resonated beyond American borders as a symbol of Black excellence and perseverance. Similarly, Muhammad Ali's global appeal is immortalized in the Superman vs. Muhammad Ali comic book, which transcends languages and cultures to depict Ali as a universal champion for justice, courage, and humanity. As Ali once declared, "I am America. I am the part you won't recognize. But get used to me. Black, confident, cocky; my name, not yours; my religion, not yours; my goals, my own—get used to me."

Artifacts such as the Wild Style Italian Movie Poster highlight hip-hop's journey from the streets of the Bronx to becoming a global cultural phenomenon, inspiring youth movements and artistic expression worldwide. This piece, featuring legends like Grandmaster Flash and Afrika Bambaataa, underscores hip-hop's universal language of resistance, creativity, and community-building. As Afrika Bambaataa remarked, "Hip-hop is not just about music. It's a culture, a movement that brings people together."

The items in this collection also emphasize the power of cross-cultural exchange. Whether through a Swedish edition of a Muhammad Ali comic book or an Italian movie poster for a hip-hop film, these artifacts demonstrate how Black art and activism have inspired audiences far beyond their origins. They serve as bridges, connecting diverse peoples to shared struggles for justice, identity, and self-expression.

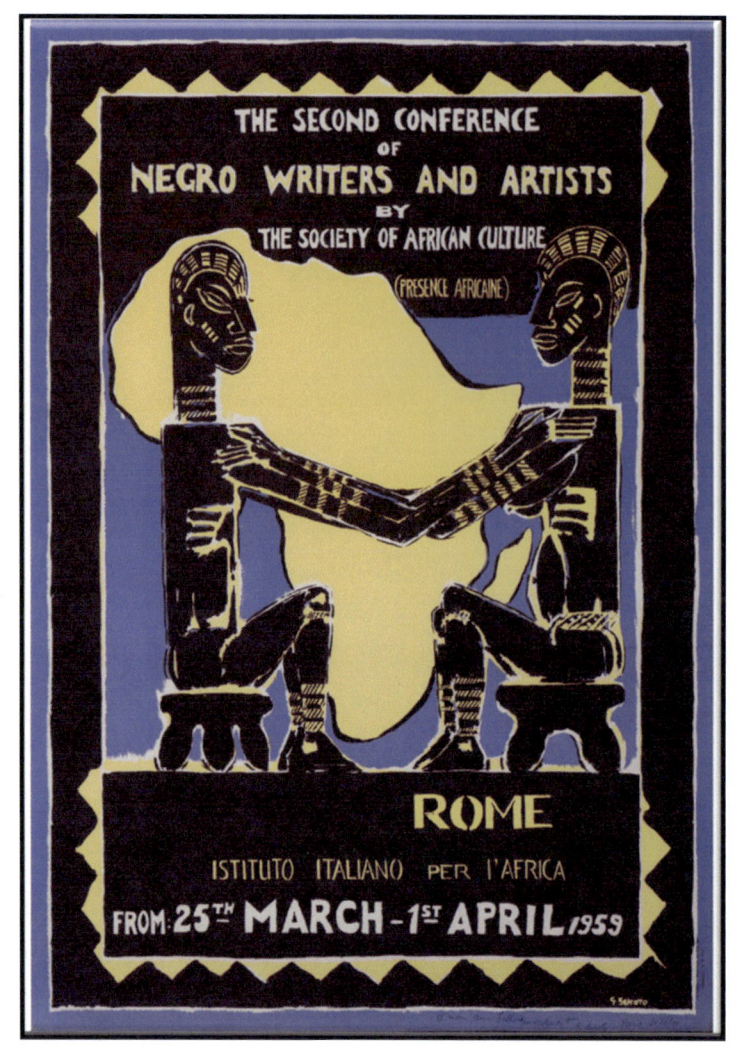

Poster for the Second Conference of Negro Writers and Artists (Rome, 1959): Highlighting Pan-African cultural dialogue.

The *Second Conference of Negro Writers and Artists* was held in Rome in 1959. The poster designed to promote the gathering reflects the intellectual and cultural fervor of the Pan-African movement during the mid-20th century. The visual design incorporates Afrocentric motifs, such as stylized depictions of African masks or patterns inspired by traditional textiles, alongside contemporary graphic elements to bridge the connection between heritage and modernity.

The conference, organized by the Société Africaine de Culture, brought together influential Black thinkers, writers, and artists from across Africa and the diaspora. Figures such as Léopold Sédar Senghor, Aimé Césaire, Frantz Fanon, and James Baldwin attended, discussing the intersections of art, literature, politics, and identity in the context of colonialism, post-colonial independence movements, and cultural liberation.

The poster not only served as a promotional tool but also symbolized the spirit of solidarity and intellectual exchange among Black creatives and activists during a transformative period in global history. Today, it stands as an artifact of the cultural renaissance that empowered generations to reclaim narratives and assert the artistic and political agency of the African diaspora.

Harlem Hellfighters photo (Post-WWI): Honoring the valor of the 369th Infantry Regiment.

This stereoview, captures the historic parade of the 369th Infantry Regiment, famously known as the Harlem Hellfighters, as they marched triumphantly up Fifth Avenue in New York City on February 17, 1919. The parade marked their return from World War I and served as a celebration of their extraordinary bravery and contributions on the battlefield. The stereoview format, a popular medium for creating three-dimensional imagery, provides a vivid and layered depiction of the moment, allowing viewers to immerse themselves in the grandeur of the event.

The Harlem Hellfighters, an all-Black regiment, spent an unprecedented 191 days on the front lines, more than any other American unit, and earned numerous commendations for their valor, including the French Croix de Guerre for their fearless service. Despite facing systemic racism and segregation within the U.S. military and at home, the soldiers of the 369th distinguished themselves as one of the most formidable fighting units of the war.

The parade began at 23rd Street, proceeded along Fifth Avenue, and culminated in Harlem, symbolizing not only the soldiers' military accomplishments but also the broader aspirations of African Americans for equality and recognition. Thousands of spectators of all races lined the streets to honor the regiment, creating a moment of unity and pride amidst a nation still grappling with racial division.

This stereoview provides an invaluable glimpse into a pivotal moment in history, capturing the energy and pride of the day while also reminding us of the resilience and courage of the Harlem Hellfighters. Their triumphant return and public recognition stand as a testament to their sacrifice and a milestone in the ongoing struggle for racial justice and equality in America.

SOARING BEYOND BARRIERS: HONORING THE TUSKEGEE AIRMEN.

This artifact is a commemorative medallion honoring the Tuskegee Airmen, a pioneering group of African American pilots who served with distinction during World War II. The medallion features the embossed profiles of three airmen, representing their bravery, skill, and contribution to the war effort, framed by the years "1941" and "1949," marking the span of their service. Below the profiles, a majestic eagle in flight symbolizes their role in breaking barriers and achieving excellence despite systemic racism and discrimination. The words "Tuskegee Airmen" arch prominently above the figures, serving as a tribute to their enduring legacy as trailblazers in military aviation and civil rights.

One of the most notable Tuskegee Airmen was Benjamin O. Davis Jr., the first African American general in the United States Air Force, who led the 332nd Fighter Group during World War II. A famous quote by Tuskegee Airman Roscoe Brown underscores their legacy:

"We proved that we could fly in combat and protect the bombers, and we set the stage for integration in the armed forces."

These commemorative medallions were issued in 2007 to honor the Tuskegee Airmen with the Congressional Gold Medal, one of the highest civilian awards in the United States. This medallion reflects the courage, excellence, and determination of these heroes, whose accomplishments continue to inspire future generations.

A RED TAIL HERO: LIEUTENANT COLONEL ALEXANDER JEFFERSON.

    This image features Lieutenant Colonel Alexander Jefferson, a distinguished Tuskegee Airman and author of *Red Tail Free*, with his handwritten signature. As a member of the 332nd Fighter Group, known as the "Red Tails," Jefferson flew numerous combat missions during World War II. In 1944, he was shot down over enemy territory and captured, spending several months as a prisoner of war in Germany. Despite enduring the harsh realities of captivity, Jefferson's resilience and dedication to his mission stand as a testament to the courage and determination of the Tuskegee Airmen.

    The personalized signature on this book cover adds a unique, historical connection to his story, symbolizing his enduring legacy as a trailblazer in American military and civil rights history. His contributions remind us of the sacrifices made by the Tuskegee Airmen in their fight for justice, equality, and the right to serve their country with honor.

120

FÖLJ TIDERNAS MATCH
FÖR ATT RÄDDA JORDEN
Stålmannen
MOT
MUHAMMAD ALI
EVERLAST
491-01

Muhammad Ali vs. Superman Comic Book (1978): Showcasing Ali's universal appeal.

This is a Swedish edition of the iconic 1978 comic book *Superman vs. Muhammad Ali*, titled *Stålmannen mot Muhammad Ali* ("Superman against Muhammad Ali"). The text on the cover, written in Swedish, translates to "Follow the fight of the ages to save Earth." This graphic novel was published in several languages to reach a global audience, underscoring Muhammad Ali's status as an international figure and cultural icon.

The story features an epic collaboration between two legends—Muhammad Ali, the world-famous heavyweight boxing champion, and Superman, the beloved superhero. In the plot, an alien species threatens Earth with invasion unless a champion can be chosen to fight their greatest warrior. Muhammad Ali and Superman, each asserting their right to represent humanity, face off in the boxing ring in a dramatic contest that determines who will go on to defend the planet.

The comic was more than just an imaginative crossover—it was a bold statement about Muhammad Ali's stature as a global hero and symbol of justice. By the time of its release, Ali had already cemented his legacy as a sports legend, civil rights activist, and outspoken critic of the Vietnam War. Pairing him with Superman represented a melding of real-life heroism and fictional superheroics, emphasizing Ali's role as a defender of humanity both inside and outside the ring.

The comic also serves as a fascinating cultural artifact of the late 1970s, reflecting the intersections of sports, politics, and popular culture. It features a crowd of spectators that includes prominent figures of the time, from political leaders to celebrities and even comic book creators.

Today, *Superman vs. Muhammad Ali* remains a highly collectible piece of memorabilia, cherished not only by comic book fans but also by those who celebrate Ali's legacy and the social impact of his career. This Swedish edition highlights the global appeal of both Ali and Superman, transcending national and linguistic boundaries to deliver a story of resilience, unity, and heroism.

Wild Style Italian Movie Poster (1982): Highlighting hip-hop's global influence.

This is an original Italian movie poster for the iconic 1982 film *Wild Style*, directed by Charles Ahearn. The film is widely regarded as the first hip-hop motion picture and is celebrated for its authentic portrayal of hip-hop culture during its formative years. Featuring elements such as breakdancing, graffiti, rap, electric boogie, and scratching, *Wild Style* captures the essence of the South Bronx hip-hop scene and its influential pioneers.

The poster's bold and vibrant design prominently displays the film's title in graffiti-style lettering, set against a gritty urban backdrop that reflects the artistic energy of the era. The central imagery highlights dynamic breakdancers in mid-performance, symbolizing the athleticism and creativity central to hip-hop culture.

Beneath the artwork, the credits list legendary figures such as Grandmaster Flash, Fab 5 Freddy, Grand Mixer DST, Afrika Bambaataa, and the South Bronx City Breakers, whose performances helped define hip-hop as a global movement. The Italian text adds an international flavor, underscoring the film's impact beyond the United States and its role in bringing hip-hop culture to a worldwide audience.

This poster is not just a piece of movie memorabilia but a historical artifact representing the birth of a cultural phenomenon that continues to resonate across the globe.

Record Mirror Magazine Cover (June 25, 1988): Spotlight on Detroit Techno and Its Legacy

This June 25, 1988, issue of *Record Mirror* marks a pivotal moment in the history of electronic music, highlighting the rise of Detroit techno with a feature on the "new dance sound of Detroit." The article spotlighted the genre's pioneering Black artists, including Juan Atkins, Derrick May, and Kevin Saunderson, collectively known as the "Belleville Three." These innovators transformed the industrial rhythms of Detroit into a futuristic sound that would lay the foundation for the global electronic dance music movement.

The cultural significance of this feature inspired the documentary "God Said Give 'Em Drum Machines", directed by Kristian R. Hill. Premiering at the 2022 Tribeca Festival, the film explores the origins of Detroit techno, weaving together archival footage, interviews, and personal narratives to celebrate the genre's roots. It highlights how the socio-economic challenges of Detroit shaped its music and how the city became a beacon for innovation in electronic sound.

This magazine serves as a time capsule, capturing the moment when Detroit techno began its ascent to international acclaim. Paired with Hill's documentary, the legacy of Detroit techno is preserved and celebrated, reminding the world of its profound impact on music and culture. Together, the magazine and film underscore Detroit's indelible role in shaping the future of global music.

30 YEARS OF PHOTOGRAPHIC MEMORIES

126

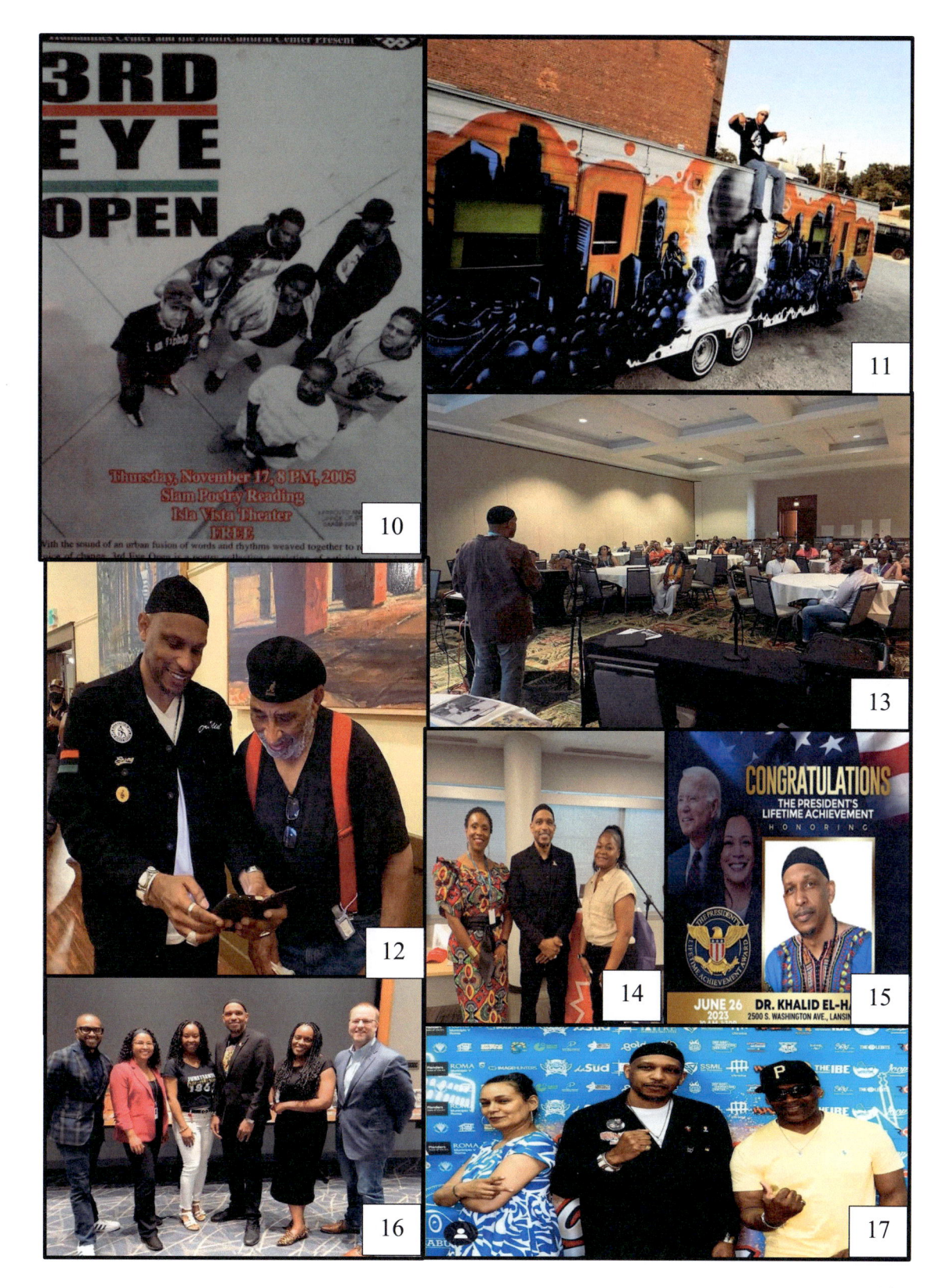

127

25

26

27

28

29

30

31

32

128

129

Chuck D ✓ @MrChuckD · 10 Feb

For BHM & beyond Please follow the great works of Dr KhalidElHakim frm Detroit @BH101MM Brother is one of the first&foremost archivists historians of Hiphop culture with his mobile museums & libraries.

130

131

59

60

61

62

63

64

65

66

67

68

133

69

70

THETA

71

FELLOW COLLECTORS OF BLACK HISTORY

Ferris State Bulldogs are EVERYWHERE!

136

MORE FSU BULLDOGS!!!

137

96

97

98

99

100

101

138

102

103

104

105

106

107

139

108

109

110

111

112

113

140

PHOTO CAPTIONS

1. The only known photo of me at the Million Man March. It was taken by my cousin Jerome Sims.
2. Proof and I on the Heidleberg Project for a rally to support the 10th anniversary of the Million Man March.
3. Baba Malik, Professor Griff, Sam Greenlee and I at the Black Star Community Bookstore in Detroit.
4. Dr. Nathan Hare, Father of Black Studies, in Oakland, CA. (Photo by Dr. Frederick Douglass Dixon)
5. Omar Hyatt and I at a Juneteenth event in Port Huron, MI sponsored by the NAACP.
6. Noni Causey of the BEAM organization and the rest of my Portland, OR family.
7. My former high school English teacher and revolutionary, Shushanna Shakur.
8. Ret. Lt. Col. Lawrence Millben, Dr. David Milburn, Lawrence Millben, Jr., Dr. Roberta Wright, wife of Dr. Charles Wright and I at the statue of The Underground Railroad.
9. Press photo for Amsterdam author Christine Otten's for her book Als Casablanca. (Photo by: Marco Bakker)
10. 3rd Eye Open Poetry Collective who I managed for several years
11. The Black History 101 Mobile Museum also known as The Hip Hop Mobile Museum. (Photo by Doug Coombe)
12. Kent Ford, founder of the Black Panther Party in Portland, OR.
13. Conducting a workshop at the NCORE conference in Honolulu, Hawaii.
14. Juneteenth program in Atlanta.
15. Flyer for my Presidential Lifetime Achievement Award.
16. Juneteenth celebration at Flagstar Bank headquarters in Troy, MI.
17. Martha Diaz, Tony Wesley, and I received an award at the Hip Hop Cine Fest in Rome, Italy for the documentary film Living Proof.
18. Minister Louis Farrakhan looking through some rare letters and photos from the archive of the Black History 101 Mobile Museum at a private meeting at the office of Atty. Gregory Reed in Detroit.
19. A family engaged in the Black History 101 Mobile Museum experience at The Alberta House in Portland, OR.
20. Speaking to some young folk at the Detroit Doll Show.
21. A Black history presentation and exhibit at Stellantis headquarters.
22. Meeting with Minister Farrakhan at the office of Atty. Gregory Reed.
23. High schoolers walking through an exhibit in Oberlin, OH.
24. Speaking to some youth about to walk through the exhibit at Xavier University in Cincinnati, OH.
25. The Black History Kick Off for the City of Southfield. Kafani Cisse, James Muhammad, Keeli Lackey, Fred Saffold, Professor Griff, Duminie Deporres and I.
26. Professor Griff and I with Umoja students at Diablo Valley College.
27. Founder of the Detroit Doll Show, Sandra Epps, Professor Griff and I.

28. At NYC Culture Con.
29. NCORE with Byrant Smith, Lasana Hotep, and Davey D.
30. KRS One visiting the Black History 101 Mobile Museum.
31. Short talk at the Idlewild International Film Festival.
32. ISNA Convention in Detroit.
33. Black History Month lecture and exhibit at First AME Church of Manassas.
34. Sharif Liwaru and I at the Malcolm X Memorial Foundation.
35. Khalilah Ali speaking to children at an exhibit in Chicago.
36. Speaking to students at Nsoroma Institute in Detroit.
37. Detroit Historian, Jamon Jordan and I at Yusef Bunchy Shakur's Urban Network.
38. Group photo of Detroit historians including Jamon Jordan, Craig Huckaby, Kwasi Akwamu, Yolanda Jack, David Rambeau, and Ken Coleman.
39. Minister Malik Shabazz and I.
40. Professor Griff speaking to students in Portland, OR.
41. Visitors to the MLK Day exhibit at the University of Michigan-Ann Arbor.
42. Black History Month lecture at Ferris State University.
43. Attorney and major collector Gregory Reed, Mike Ellison and I at the Black History Month Kick-Off in Southfield, MI.
44. Petty Propolis Art Festival and Retreat in Idlewild, MI.
45. Sam Greenlee, Professor Griff and Detroit Job Corps students preparing to renovate the Black History 101 Mobile Museum trailer.
46. The Last Poets visiting the Detroit Job Corps when I was a teacher.
47. That time Chuck D tweeted about my work!
48. Chuck D and Detroit hip hop pioneer Awesome Dre visiting the BH101MM trailer.
49. Dr. Amer Ahmed one of the biggest supporters of the Black History 101 Mobile Museum who was responsible for our first booking on a college campus.
50. The exterior of the Black History 101 Mobile Museum trailer.
51. My daughters Keisha, BreAna, and Khalilah.
52. Cover of my children's book, Khalid and Khalilah's ABC's of Black History.
53. My Speak Out Agency family at NCORE in Portland, OR.
54. Lasana Hotep, Dr. Shakti Butler, Dr. Amer Ahmed, and Bryant Smith.
55. DJ Kuttin Kandi, Olmeca, Amer, and Jasiri X.
56. Dr. Frederick Douglas Dixon, director of the Center for Black Studies at Radford University in Vi.rginia.
57. Dr. LaGarrett King, Shantelle Browning-Morgan and I at the Teaching Black History Conference.
58. Olmeca, Rosa Clemente, Dr. Mike Benitez, and Dr. Amer Ahmed.
59. Dr. Yusef Shakur and I at UNC-Greensboro.
60. Motown legend Martha Reeves at the Detroit City Council Black History Month Program.
61. On set with journalist Soledad O'Brien and J.R. Smith for a Toyota sponsored podcast.
62. Jessica Care Moore, Piper Carter and Miz Korona receiving an award.

63. Photo shoot with Metro Times with photographer Doug Coombe.
64. Hip hop artist Champtown at a screening of The Untold Story of Detroit Hip Hop and BH101MM exhibit at Western Michigan University.
65. Students at Jefferson High School in Portland.
66. Students walking through an exhibit at IUPUI in Indiana.
67. Elementary school students excited to read Khalid and Khalilah's ABC's of Black History
68. Excited group of youth who just experienced the Black History 101 Mobile Museum.
69. My first exhibit at a HBCU was Rust College in Mississppi.
70. Students visit an exhibit at Santa Clara University.
71. NCORE photo with Olmeca, Natalia Pinto, Amer Ahmed, Ernie Paniccioli, Jasiri X, Aisha Fukashima and others.
72. Delbert Richardson of The Unspoken Truths visits the BH101MM in Seattle.
73. Philip Merrill of Nanny Jack and Co. visits the BH101MM at South Piedmont College.
74. Journalist and collector Kahn Davison visits the BH101MM at MOCAD in Detroit.
75. Gene Alexander Peters of Sankofa Exhibit and Leonard Davis visit the BH101MM at the Lincoln Center in NY.
76. Michael Carter and colleague host the BH101MM at Sinclair College in Dayton, OH.
77. Professor Griff and I stop in on collector Eric Majette's exhibit in Atlanta.
78. Rocky Bucano, Founder of The Hip Hop Museum and Paradise Gray in The Bronx receiving a donation of a DJ Kool Herc belt buckle from me.
79. Archivist Lisbet Tellefesen visit the BH101MM at Skyline College in San Bruno, CA.
80. Ferris alumni Keeli Lackey and Sabrina Frazier visit the BH101MM in West Bloomfield, MI.
81. Ferris alumni Eric Weeks visits the BH101MM in Atlanta.
82. Ferris alumni Lisa Alexander visits the BH101MM in Lansing, MI.
83. Ferris alumni Craig Smith and wife Amy visit the BH101MM in Colorado.
84. One of my Ferris State mentors Terri Houston meets with Omari and I while we're in Portland, OR.
85. Ferris alumni Monte Brown visits the BH101MM in Flint
86. Ferris alumni Raymond Gant speaks to a group of educators about the BH101MM in St. Louis.
87. Ferris alumni Todd Ebersole visits the BH101MM Portland Community College in Portland, OR.
88. Ferris Alumni Stan and Kim Schely, Twanna Wade, and Shannon Brown visit the BH101MM in Roswell, GA.
89. Ferris alumni Evette Smith at the Black Wall Street exhibit in Atlanta.
90. Ferris alumni Rob Carpenter visits the BH101MM in Ashville, NC.
91. Ferris alumni Matt Chaney and former Ferris professor Oliver Bridges with Dick Gregory in DC.
92. Ferris alumni Robert Shumake and Jessica Care Moore visiting the BH101MM at the African World Festival in Detroit.
93. Ferris alumni Mike Lavely in Reno.

94. Former Ferris State professor and one of my mentors Dr. Jimmy Cornett.
95. Ferris alumni Luke Wycoff visits the BH101MM at Regis University in Denver.
96. Jessica Ramirez and crew at Tacoma Community College.
97. Kolbe Cole of Trails Ministries in Beaver Falls, PA.
98. Chrysler 300 designer and Chief Design Officer of Stellantis, Ralph Giles visiting the BH101MM at Stellantis.
99. Middle school students visitng the BH101MM in Oberlin OH.
100. Champtown and wife Keysha, Khalilah el-Hakim, Dr. Wallace, Dr. Gus Calbert, Tasleem el-Hakim, and Shimonta Dickerson at Western Michigan University.
101. BH101MM exhibit at Avalon Village in Highland Park with Griff, Jessica Care Moore, and Mama Shu.
102. Leda Watts visits the BH101MM at Avalon Village.
103. Kevin Collins visits the BH101MM in Lansing, MI
104. Paul James of Duke University.
105. Grand daughters, Nevaeh and Isaly visiting the BH101MM in Arlington, TX.
106. Ralph Carter aka Michael Evans of the hit TV show *Good Times* signing autographs at the BH101MM.
107. Shá Duncan-Smith at Swarthmore College with guests Umar bin Hassan and MC Sha Rock.
108. Print ad for Toyota's *Need a Nudge* campaign.
109. Creative director of Toyota's Need a Nudge campaign, Corey Seaton.
110. Print ad for Toyota's *Need a Nudge* campaign.
111. Black Educators Rock Conferece founder, Dr. Melissa Chester.
112. Students wait in line to have copies of their book autographed
113. Excited youth in Ypsilanti, MI receive copies of *Khalilah and Khalid's ABC's of Black History*.

BLACK HISTORY 101 MOBILE MUSEUM FLYERS

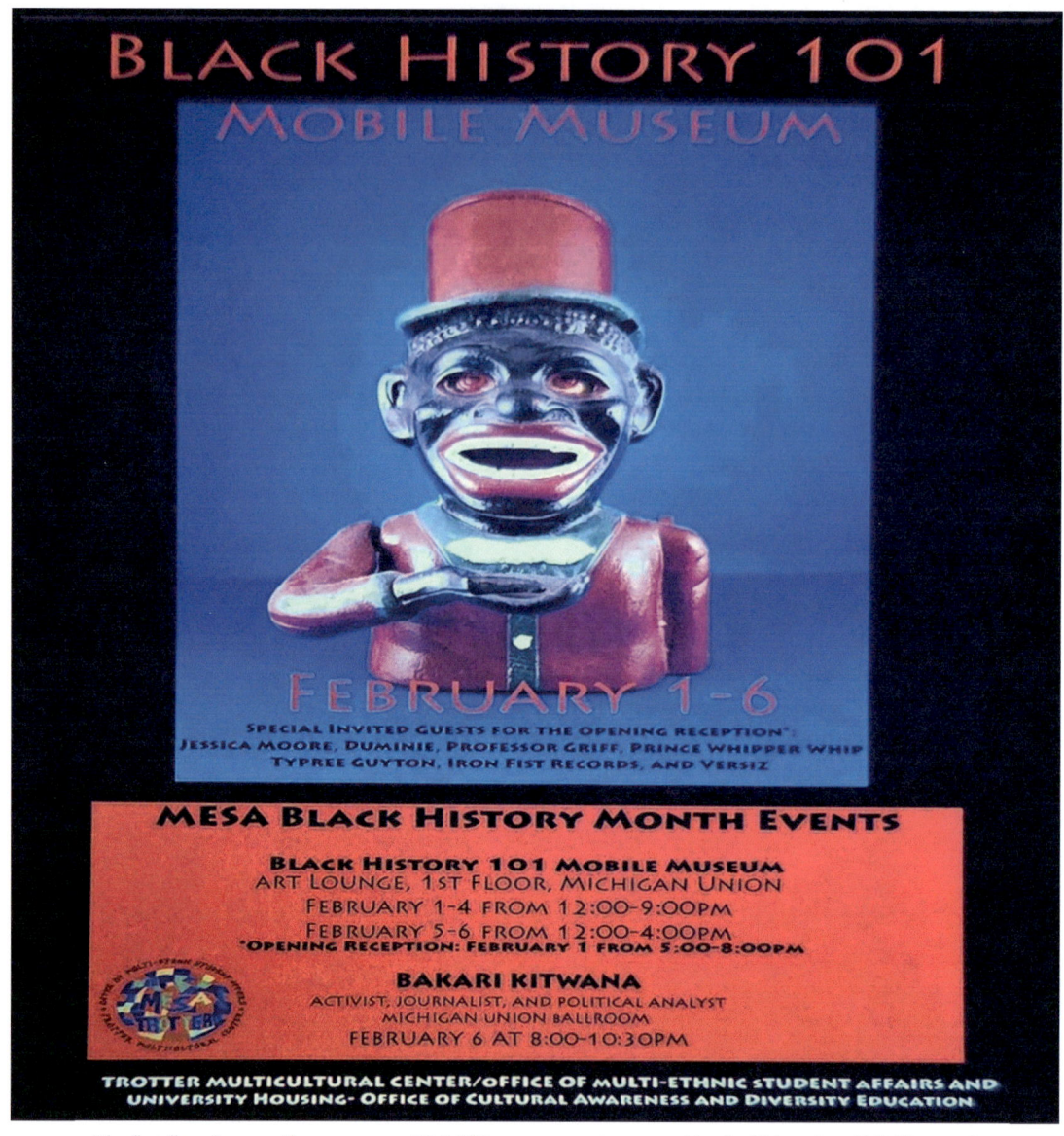

The first flyer from a college campus exhibit. This was an event sponsored by the University of Michigan under the directorship of my good friend, Dr. Amer Ahmed in 2007.

LAMAR UNIVERSITY
BLACK HISTORY 101 MOBILE MUSEUM
2/15/2021 | Setzer Student Center Atrium | 12 - 5 p.m.
With a presentation by professor and museum curator, Dr. Khalid El-Hakim
DRINKING FOUNTAIN
WHITE
COLORED
Black History 101 Mobile Museum
Tuesday, February 11th
Visit the BRIDGE Center between 1:00-6:00PM to view original artifacts of Black memorabilia from throughout history
THE BLACK MASS COMMUNICATION PROJECT PRESENTS
BLACK HISTORY 101 MOBILE MUSEUM
MONDAY APRIL 22ND
FINE ARTS CENTER LOBBY 3-8PM
JOIN BMCP AS WE TOUR OVER 150 ORIGINAL ARTIFACTS OF MEMORABILIA DATING FROM THE TRANS-ATLANTIC SLAVE TRADE TO HIP HOP CULTURE.
HOSTED BY KHALID EL-HAKIM
BLACK HISTORY 101 TRAVELING MUSEUM
WEDNESDAY, MARCH 16 | 10 A.M. - 3 P.M.
High Library - 1st Floor
Attend a lecture on The Black Museum Movement in America at 12:30 p.m.!
Black History 101 Mobile Museum
Event Highlights
How to Participate
AUGUST 5 | 12-5 P.M.
FLOYD B. SIMMONS CENTER
Martin Luther King Jr. Day
SPEAKER
BLACK HISTORY 101 MOBILE MUSEUM
Khalid el-Hakim, founder and curator
Spokane Community College
BLACK HISTORY MOBILE MUSEUM
FEBRUARY 1ST
10 AM - 3 PM
ATRIUM
SPECIAL PRESENTATION BY DR. EL-HAKIM
12:30 PM - 1:30 PM
BLACK HISTORY 101 Mobile Museum
LIVE EXHIBIT
FOUNDER AND CURATOR DR KHALID EL-HAKIM
NATIONAL EXECUTIVE DIRECTOR PROFESSOR GRIFF
ETHICS LECTURE SERIES
FALL 2018
BLACK HISTORY 101 MOBILE MUSEUM
MUSIC OF THE MOVEMENT
TUESDAY, OCT. 15
KALAMAZOO VALLEY COMMUNITY COLLEGE
TEXAS TOWNSHIP CAMPUS | ROOM 4240
LECTURE
DROP-IN MUSEUM HOURS
Hosted by The Association Of Black Collegians
The Black History 101 Mobile Museum
Wintergreen Gardens
McGarvey Commons
February 19th
Penn State Behrend
SAT. MAY 14TH @ 11 AM 3 PM
NEW BLACK WALL STREET MARKET
QUESday: Omegas in the Laboratory Disp
KUC 2nd Floor, 11:00 a.m. to 1:00 p.m.
Wednesday, February 23
Black History Mobile Museum
KUC Knoll, 9:00 a.m. to 5:00 p.m.
Sponsored by Black History Month Committee
Contact: Vincent Windrow at 898-2831 or vwindrow@mtsu.edu
Dr. Quito Swan's Black Power in Bermuda
The Black History 101 Mobile Museum is coming to campus!
UNIVERSITY OF MICHIGAN-DEARBORN
Tuesday, February 2
Wednesday, February 3
MUSIC ON THE ONE'S & TWO'S BY
AFRICAN AMERICAN MUSIC APPRECIATION MONTH
Celebrates
MC SHA ROCK
Cultural Day
HOSTED BY ANDY KING & RAH DIGGA
SATURDAY JUNE 5 2021
GUN HILL PLAYGROUND

Portland Community College
Multicultural Centers Present:
Black History 101
"It Takes a Nation of Millions"
February 24, 2009
12noon-1PM
Bldg. 3 TLC Rm.
(to the right of the coffee bar)
Don't miss out!
Professor Griff
An American Rapper, Outspoken activist and former member of hip hop group "Public Enemy".
Khalid El-Hakim
An avid collector of African-American memorabilia and has enough artifacts to stock a small Museum.
For more information contact Equity Ambassadors in the Multicultural Center.
Email: thrive@pcc.edu
Phone: 503-614-7435

BLACK HISTORY 101
MOBILE MUSEUM
OCTOBER 1ST
10AM-5PM
THE GREAT ROOM
The Godfathers of Hip Hop celebrate their 50th Anniversary traveling with the Black History 101 Mobile Museum!
KHALID EL-HAKIM
FEAT.
THE LAST POETS
7PM-9PM
JCSU BALLROOMS
The Center
GRI
Joe Crowley Student Union
If you require a reasonable accommodation in order to participate in this event, please contact Joseph Lykes two weeks prior to the event at 775-682-8008 or jlykes@unr.edu.

KHALID EL-HAKIM
BLACK HISTORY 101
MOBILE MUSEUM
NECESSARY!
FRIDAY
FEBRUARY 28TH
10AM - 5PM
IRC CORRIDOR
FERRIS STATE UNIVERSITY
Office of Multicultural Student Services
Exhibit is free and open to the public
If you have a disability and need assistance to attend, contact OMSS at (231) 591-2617 at least 72 hours in advance.

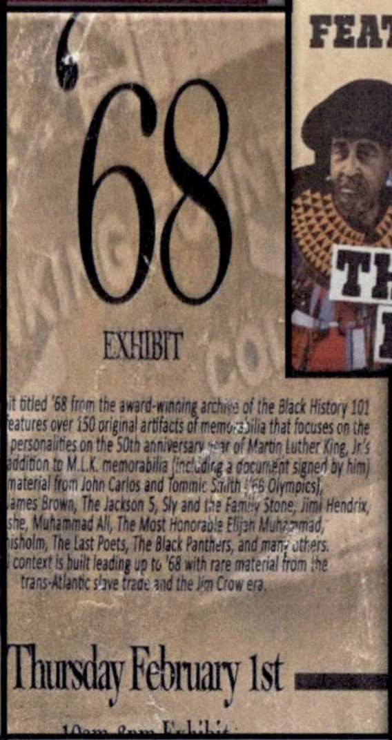
'68
EXHIBIT
Thursday February 1st

Historia Negra 101 Exhibiciones
con el Dr. el-Hakim
Jueves, 2 de febrero | 1:00 – 7:00 pm
Viernes, 3 de febrero | 10:00 am – 4:00 pm
Biblioteca Principal – 111 Library St NE

PROFESSOR GRIFF
"It Takes A Nation Of Millions"
Public Enemy is celebrating their 20 anniversary of It Takes a Nation of Millions release .There is no list in any American book or magazine that doesn't list the ground breaking album It Takes a Nation of Millions as one of the top albums in American popular music. Released in 1988, Professor Griff is going to address the social, political, and global impact of one of the most influential albums ever made.
Wednesday, October 15, 2008
7pm
Rankin Student Center
Dome Room

Saturday 12p - 4p
May 17, 2008
Omaha North High
36th & Ames
Featuring
2008 Cultural Festival
Malcolm X Celebration
FOR MORE INFORMATION GO TO WWW.MALCOLMXFOUNDATION.ORG OR CALL 1-800-645-
BLACK HISTORY 101 MOBILE MUSEUM
HIP-HOP HISTORY 101
DRINKING FOUNTAIN
WHITE
COLORED
THEME:
THE MUSIC OF THE MOVEMENT
10 AM- 3 PM DAILY
Monday, Jan 22nd & Tuesday, Jan 23rd in North Mall of CC Building on Sylvania Campus of Portland Community College
• Dr. el-Hakim will lecture on Tuesday from 1 pm - 2:50 pm in the Sylvani Multicultural Center
DISTRICT MULTICULTURAL CENTERS
FOR MORE INFORMATION, CONTACT CULTURE@PCC.EDU
UAW LOCALS 602 AND 2256
CIVIL AND HUMAN RIGHTS COMMITTEES
2017
CELEBRATE
Black History
BLACK HISTORY 101
MOBILE MUSEUM
(FOUNDED BY: KHALID EL-HAKIM)
THE BLACK HISTORY 101 MOBILE MUSEUM IS AN AWARD WINNING COLLECTION OF OVER 5,000 ORIGINAL ARTIFACTS OF BLACK MEMORABILIA.
KEYNOTE SPEAKER:
PROFESSOR GRIFF
(FROM HIP/HOP GROUP PUBLIC ENEMY)
SATURDAY FEBRUARY 18, 2017
MEET AND GREET
PROFESSOR GRIFF OF PUBLIC ENEMY
KHALID EL-HAKIM, FOUNDER
BLACK HISTORY 101 MOBILE MUSEUM
THURSDAY, MAY 29
7PM
CORONADO R AND S
SPONSORED BY:
HIP HOP CONGRESS
ON TOUR THIS FALL!!!!
FOR MORE INFO CALL
313 645-4197
TOYOTA
CULTURECON NYC 2022 PANEL OVERVIEW
PANELISTS:
Dr. Khalid el-Hakim
• Founder and curator of the Black History 101 Mobile Museum Been named the "Schomburg of the Hip-Hop generation"
• Received attention for his innovative work of exhibiting Black history outside of traditional museum spaces
Ty Hunter
• Designer, entrepreneur, and stylist
• Creator of With Passion Collection and Ty Lite
• Celebrity Stylist to Beyonce, Solange, Billy Porter and more
BLACK HISTORY 101
MOBILE MUSEUM
@ Oak Park Public Library
JUNETEENTH
19 JUNE: 4 PM - 7 PM
KEYNOTE ADDRESS: 6 PM
CURATOR DR. KHALID EL-HAKIM
BLACK HISTORY MONTH
FEBRUARY 2023
www.dvc.edu/black-history
Student Equity Speaker Series - Speaker: Malkia Devich Cyril
Film Screening - Living Legacy of Black Panther Party
Black History 101 Mobile Museum: Curated by Khalid el-Hakim
Wikipedia Edit-A-Thon
Social Justice in collaboration with Ethnic Studies - Speaker: Tiffani Marie
DVC
DIABLO VALLEY COLLEGE
TTSD FACS'S PRESENTS
BLACK HISTORY 101 MOBILE MUSEUM
VIRTUAL EVENT
RSVP HERE
http://bit.ly/TTSDMBHM
WEDNESDAY, MARCH 3
5:30PM-7:00PM
Founded by Dr. Khalid el-Hakim, the Black History 101 Mobile Museum is an award winning collection of over 10,000 original artifacts of Black memorabilia dating from the trans-Atlantic slave trade era to hip-hop culture. As the nation's premiere Black history traveling exhibit, the Black History 101 Mobile Museum has visited 40 states sharing "ourstory" at over 500 institutions reaching tens of thousands of visitors in diverse spaces.
FEB 1ST 9AM - 2PM ATRIUM
BLACK HISTORY 101
MOBILE MUSEUM
DR. KHALID EL-HAKIM, FOUNDER
PRESENTATION AT 12:30PM

In the news...

Kwasi Akwamu, a journalist for *The Michigan Citizen*, wrote the first article about my work on May 20, 2002. At the time, the project was called *The Bell Collection*, named in honor of my family.

The Detroit News
SERVING MICHIGAN SINCE 1873

2A The Detroit News | Sunday, June 5, 2005

Neal Rubin

To never forget, activist saves vile pieces of black history

It's a word we don't put in the paper, and a word Khalid el-Hakim would just as soon wipe from everyone's vocabulary, no matter their race or level of hipness. But he can show you a mechanical bank where it's cast in iron on the back.

El-Hakim is black and active and committed, and he offers compelling reasons to preserve this sort of thing instead of burying it in a landfill. "If you destroy it," he contends, "there's no evidence it ever existed."

So he demonstrates how you put a coin on the outstretched hand of a cartoonish black man in a top hat and flip a lever. The man's eyes go white and the coin disappears through his gigantic red lips, and isn't it fun, kids?

C'mon, you say. The bank is probably 100 years old. No one would sell that today. Except that el-Hakim can reach into another display case at his home in Highland Park and grab a yellow cardboard box with a tube of toothpaste inside.

It was sold in Southeast Asia within the past 10 years, he says. There's another black man in another top hat on the box, and above him is the brand name of the fine product within: A slur maybe half a level less startling than the one on the bank.

El-Hakim, 35, teaches middle school social studies to kids in Detroit with what educators gently call "behavioral and attendance challenges." He hopes to keep doing it next year, even if last week's mail brought a layoff notice.

That's another story, though. Today's subject is why, on a dreary afternoon two Sundays ago, el-Hakim and his friend Geoffrey Devereaux drove to Howell for the estate sale of one of the leading flaming racists in Michigan history.

Part of the reason Devereaux went is that el-Hakim's friend Proof, the well-known rapper, wouldn't. Financially, "I got your back," el-Hakim says Proof told him. When it came to sitting next to him, Proof said, "No way," and Devereaux understands the response.

Khalid el-Hakim holds a Nation of Islam newspaper from his collection, pieces of which have been displayed in Detroit.

ly Klan supporters, only five of them black. "It was macabre."

As for el-Hakim's primary interest, he showed up wanting some of that natty Ku Klux Klan sportswear. But really, all your average robe and hood tells you is that whoever wore it was afraid to show his face.

His interest is black history, so by the time some self-identified Klan-sympathizing goofball spent $6,000 on Robert Miles' two black robes, el-Hakim had changed direction.

For a total of $250, el-Hakim says, he bought something far more valuable: A glimpse inside the old Grand Dragon's head.

There was a black-and-white photo Miles liked enough to have framed of himself with a burning cross. Some books by black authors a librarian might catalog under "revolutionary," including "War in America" by Brother Imari. A box of Anti-Defamation League reports on potentially menacing organizations like Miles' own.

Best of all, el-Hakim now owns Miles' scrapbook — a newspaper clipping play-by-play of Klan activities or things the Klan probably wished it had thought of, like bombing school buses in Pontiac in 1971 and tarring and feathering a pointedly tolerant high school principal in Ypsilanti the same year.

"If I could admire something about a Klan person," el-Hakim says, "he was very well-read." Knowing what Miles was reading can only help a historian understand what he was thinking.

El-Hakim calls his assembled artifacts The Bell Collection. His name was Stan Bell until he converted to Islam 11 years ago, "and my mom was not too happy with the name change, so it is in honor of my family."

These days, his mom cheerfully refers to him as Khalid,

and she can tell you most everywhere pieces of the collection have been displayed, among them Wayne State, the Detroit Job Corps and the Charles H. Wright Museum of African American History.

To inquire about an exhibit, e-mail newrisingsun99@yahoo.com. Much of the material is arresting without being appalling: Mattel's first black Barbie, known simply as "Black Barbie." Or a book he found at a thrift store, inscribed to the previous owner by Rosa Parks. Or the New York Daily News edition covering the Million Man March in October 1995, an event he attended and which spurred him to expand his small trove and find ways to bring it to the public.

Much, however, is dumbfoundingly offensive. He and artist Tyree Guyton are fiddling with plans for a motor-home-based exhibit. Its name will be deliberately jarring, just like the illustrated postcard in a rack on his mantle that shows a black man stealing a chicken. "A bird in de han," he's saying, "am worth two in the coop." "I want to open people's eyes to pay attention to this stuff," el-Hakim says. "You can't get over it until you deal with it."

There's another postcard, Depression-era, from Dover, Del., on which a pudgy, shirtless black man is chained to a post. A white man in a sport coat and straw hat stands behind him holding a whip. A crowd is gathered to watch, and most of the spectators are children.

"Some of these kids are still alive," el-Hakim says. Some of them might have even owned that cast-iron bank. He can't change that, but maybe he can help them wish they hadn't.

Neal Rubin appears Sunday, Tuesday, Wednesday and Friday. Reach him at (313) 222-1874 or nrubin@detnews.com.

Neal Rubin wrote about my experience attending the Klan auction in Howell, Michigan. Many readers took offense, and rightly so, to the contrast between the article's title, *'To never forget, activist saves vile pieces of Black history,'* and the photo they chose to use—a picture of me holding a *Muhammad Speaks* newspaper featuring Muhammad Ali on the cover. There is nothing vile about Muhammad Ali, and the image sent a conflicting and misleading message.

150

THE BOWDOIN ORIENT

ARTS & ENTERTAINMENT

Mobile museum teaches black history through artifacts

By Conrad Li
Orient Staff

---

yes! Solutions Journalism

His Traveling Museum Is Bringing Black History to a Town Near You

PITTSBURGH Jewish Chronicle

PRESERVING HISTORY / BLACK HISTORY 101 MOBILE MUSEUM

Mobile Museum artifacts are tools for telling stories

Khalid el-Hakim's mobile museum began with a collection of artifacts. Thousands of acquisitions later, he's still searching for one thing: dialogue

BY ADAM REINHERZ
10 January 2022, 12:56 pm

BLACK ENTERPRISE — WEALTH FOR LIFE

by Daron Pressley October 11, 2017

BE MODERN MAN: MEET 'MR. BLACK HISTORY 101' KHALID EL-HAKIM

2A — Thursday, February 7, 2008

MONDAY: In Other Ivory Towers TUESDAY: Arbor Anecdote

LEARNING BLACK HISTORY

Detroit-based musician Omari Barksdale (right) talk at an exhibit celebrating the late musician J Dilla at the Black History 101 Mobile Museum. The museum, currently on display in the Michigan Union, contains black culture memorabilia owned by Khalid el-Hakim, a schoolteacher in Detroit.

CLEVELAND Jewish News — We Stand with Israel — 60 YEARS

Black history museum founder discusses role of artifacts in race, racism

BECKY RASPE
braspe@cjn.org Posted Jan 18, 2022 at 3:00 PM Updated Jan 19, 2022 at 12:43 PM

HOUR DETROIT

Things to Do

Explore Black History at the Black History 101 Mobile Museum

Detroit native Dr. Khalid el-Hakim founded the Black History 101 Mobile Museum to highlight the Black experience in America with historic artifacts, photos and more.

By Darlene A. White · February 7, 2023

Lansing State Journal

LOCAL

Black History mobile museum reflects 'resiliency of Black experience in America'

Matthew Dae Smith
Lansing State Journal

---

the grio

Malcolm X artifacts unearthed: Police docs and more found among belongs of 'Shorty' Jarvis

DETROIT (AP) - Documents outlining the crime that landed Malcolm X in prison in the 1940s are among some 1,000 recently unearthed items purchased jointly by the civil rights leader's foundation...

DETROIT METRO TIMES

Black History 101 Mobile Museum debuts

How rapper Khalid El-Hakim founded his mobile black history museum

By Kahn Santori Davison

The Detroit News
SERVING MICHIGAN SINCE 1873

WAYNE COUNTY

Detroit native's traveling Black history museum stops Friday at WSU

The Black History 101 Mobile Museum was shaped by hip-hop artists, the Black consciousness movement, Million Man March and Detroit native Khalid el-Hakim. It will be on display Friday at WSU.

Kim Kozlowski
The Detroit News

EBONY

CULTURE, ENTERTAINMENT, RACE & CULTURE, THE ARTS

MOBILE MUSEUM IN DETROIT TEACHES BLACK HISTORY 101

By #TeamEBONY | February 1, 2012

Proclamation

WHEREAS: It is with great privilege and honor that we celebrate and welcome the Black History 101 Mobile Museum traveling exhibit; and

WHEREAS: Founded by Dr. Khalid el-Hakim, the Black History 101 Mobile Museum is an award-winning collection of over 10,000 original artifacts of Black memorabilia dating from the trans-Atlantic slave trade era to hip-hop culture; and

WHEREAS: Dr. el-Hakim has been called the "Schomburg of the Hip-Hop generation" because of his passionate commitment to carry on the rich tradition of the Black Museum Movement; and

WHEREAS: Dr. el-Hakim is a Michigan native, born in Detroit where he attended Detroit Public Schools and developed his love for hip-hop culture and black history as well as his aspiration to share that love with as many people as he could; and

WHEREAS: Dr. el-Hakim returned to Detroit Public Schools and has taught Social Science for over 15 years. He earned his Ph.D. in education and spreads knowledge of his culture across the nation; and

WHEREAS: Having traveled the country for 30 years combing through antique shops, flea markets, estate sales, and auctions, Dr. el-Hakim has personally acquired a diverse archive of memorabilia distinctively situating itself among the most sought after exhibits of its kind in America; and

WHEREAS: As the nation's premiere Black history traveling exhibit, the Black History 101 Mobile Museum has visited 41 states sharing "ourstory" at over 500 institutions, reaching tens of thousands of visitors in diverse spaces including colleges, K-12 schools, corporations, conferences, libraries, museums, festivals, religious institutions, and cultural events.

NOW, THEREFORE, I, Andy Schor, Mayor of the City of Lansing, by the power vested in me do hereby proclaim June 21st, 2022, as:

"Dr. Khalid el-Hakim Day"

in Lansing. I encourage all residents to join me in recognizing Dr. el-Hakim for his monumental efforts in curating this exhibit and sharing it with our residents so they may appreciate and celebrate this rich culture and history.

Given under my hand and seal this twenty-first day of June in the year two thousand and twenty-two.

Andy Schor
Mayor
City of Lansing

STATE OF MICHIGAN

SPECIAL TRIBUTE

To

KHALID EL-HAKIM

LET IT BE KNOWN, That it is with deep appreciation for the commitment, passion, and proficiency that Khalid el-Hakim has put forth on behalf of the children of Detroit that we offer this expression of our thanks and best wishes. Founder of the Black History 101 Mobile Museum, Khalid has demonstrated a dedication to the preservation of Detroit's Rich History of Arts and Culture. His work ensures children living within the region will have a promising future.

Khalid el-Hakim is an educator, music executive, and founder of the Black History 101 Mobile Museum. A vocal historian, Khalid has been described as "the hip hop generation's Arthur Schomburg."

The award winning Black History 101 Mobile Museum is a collection of over 5,000 original artifacts that spans the Black experience from slavery to hip-hop. The Museum travels to colleges and universities, K-12 schools, libraries, conferences, and cultural events across the country, exhibiting rare pieces of history, collected by Khalid el-Hakim personally.

Khalid served as Vice President of Iron Fist Records, during early millennium. During that time, he promoted and marketed Proof DeShaun Holton (1973-2006) of D12's final recording projects *Searchin' for Jerry Garcia* and *Hand 2 Hand* mixtape. In addition, el-Hakim co-produced Holton's *Take the Land* album. Khalid is the executive producer of the Detroit legendary hip-hop group 5 ELA's 2013 album titled Global Warming.

An esteemed author, Khalid published *Drum Majors for Justice* in 2012, a book of quotes by African American politicians. Later, in 2013, Khalid published the groundbreaking book entitled *The Center of the Movement: Collecting Hip Hop Memorabilia*. This book has earned Khalid national accolades, including an invitation to present the book at the Schomburg Center in Harlem.

Khalid was inducted into the national honor society of Phi Kappa Phi in 2013. He is currently a candidate to receive a Master of Arts in Socio-Cultural Studies in Education from Western Michigan University, expected for completion in May of 2014.

It is through his many accomplishments as an artist, educator, activist, and entrepreneur that he has contributed to the preservation of Detroit's Rich History of Arts & Culture, and the hope that every child will someday inherit the benefits associated with this contribution.

IN SPECIAL TRIBUTE, Therefore, This document is signed and dedicated to Khalid el-Hakim for his many accomplishments as an artist, activist and entrepreneur that he has contributed to the preservation of Detroit's Rich History of Arts and Culture, and the hope that every child will someday inherit the benefits associated with this contribution.

Thomas Stallworth, State Representative
The Seventh District

The Ninety-Seventh Legislature
At Lansing
Tuesday, November 26, 2013

THE STATE OF OKLAHOMA

Citation of Recognition

Khalid el-Hakim

Whereas, the **Black History 101 Mobile Museum**, an exhibit that includes over 7,000 original artifacts of Black memorabilia, including artifacts signed by Martin Luther King Jr., Malcolm X, Rosa Parks, George Washington Carver, Frederick Douglass, Booker T. Washington, Coretta Scott King and many others, as well as a rare slave bill of trade and shackles were presented for display at the Greenwood Cultural Center in Tulsa beginning on Sunday, July 10th, 2016. Khalid el-Hakim is partnered with Professor Griff to promote education through critical thinking, and;

Whereas, the **Black History 101 Mobile Museum** is currently on national tour and has made its way across 23 states and over 60 college campuses as well as K-12 schools, libraries, conferences and cultural events for the past 10 years, and;

Whereas, the **Black History 101 Mobile Museum** was founded by Khalid el-Hakim, a former Detroit Public School teacher and current Ph.D. student at the University of Illinois for the purpose of giving communities a unique glimpse into African American history and to experience the legacy of many iconic and notable figures from a more intimate perspective, and;

Whereas, it is proper and fitting that the Oklahoma State Legislature, acting on behalf of the citizens of Oklahoma, takes pride in extending recognition to Khalid el-Hakim for his active role in furthering racial relations and lending his voice to the dialogue concerning the challenging issues of race and educating the public with his **Black History 101 Mobile Museum**.

Now, therefore pursuant to the motion of

Representative Regina Goodwin

the Oklahoma House of Representatives extends to

Khalid el-Hakim

sincere congratulations and directs that this citation be presented.

Representative Regina Goodwin
House District 73

STATE OF MICHIGAN

SPECIAL TRIBUTE

For

The 50th Anniversary of Hip-Hop

For Impact on Music, Culture and Society

LET IT BE KNOWN, That it is a distinct privilege to commemorate the 50th Anniversary of Hip-Hop and celebrate its impact on music, culture, and society.

While all music can ignite the emotions of its audience and channel their frustrations, fears, and hopes, hip-hop has often managed to harness that power for social justice and social change. Since its inception, hip-hop has promoted individualism and unabashed expression along with messages that condemn inequality, most notably, the inequalities that affect Black communities. Over the last five decades, the genre has also inspired several country-wide debates on topics too often ignored, refusing to bend to societal constraints. Beyond its educational importance, hip-hop has been the entertainment of choice for people of all ages, engaging more individuals in art and music culture than ever before. Today, we wish to celebrate and acknowledge the importance and longevity of the hip-hop genre.

IN SPECIAL TRIBUTE, Therefore, we acknowledge the 50th Anniversary of Hip-Hop and its importance to the generations that it has inspired.

Emily E. Dievendorf, State Representative
The Seventy-Seventh District

Kara Hope, State Representative
The Seventy-Fourth District

Sam Singh, State Senator
The Twenty-Eighth District

Sarah Anthony, State Senator
The Twenty-First District

Andy Schor
Mayor of Lansing

The One Hundred and Second Legislature
At Lansing
June 26, 2023

SPIRIT OF DETROIT AWARD

is presented herewith as an expression of the
gratitude and esteem of the citizens of Detroit
to

Khalid El - Hakim, Founder
Black History 101, Mobile Museum

in recognition of exceptional achievement,
outstanding leadership and dedication to
improving the quality of life.

By the City Council
of Detroit, Michigan

Charles Pugh
COUNCIL PRESIDENT

COUNCIL PRESIDENT PRO TEM — COUNCIL MEMBER

COUNCIL MEMBER — COUNCIL MEMBER

COUNCIL MEMBER — COUNCIL MEMBER

COUNCIL MEMBER — COUNCIL MEMBER

April 28, 2012
DATE

Urban League of Detroit
& Southeastern Michigan
Since 1916
2022
Community Service Award
Presented to
Dr. Khalid el-Hakim
Founder and Curator
Black History 101 Mobile Museum
FOR OUTSTANDING LEADERSHIP,
DEDICATION AND COMPASSION
PRESENTED BY
URBAN LEAGUE OF DETROIT
& SOUTHEASTERN MICHIGAN
Guild Gala
December 10, 2022

ASALH
FREEDOM SCHOLAR
AWARD
PRESENTED TO
Dr. Khalid el-Hakim
106th ANNUAL
MEETING & VIRTUAL CONFERENCE
SEPTEMBER 28, 2021

WHAT PEOPLE ARE SAYING....

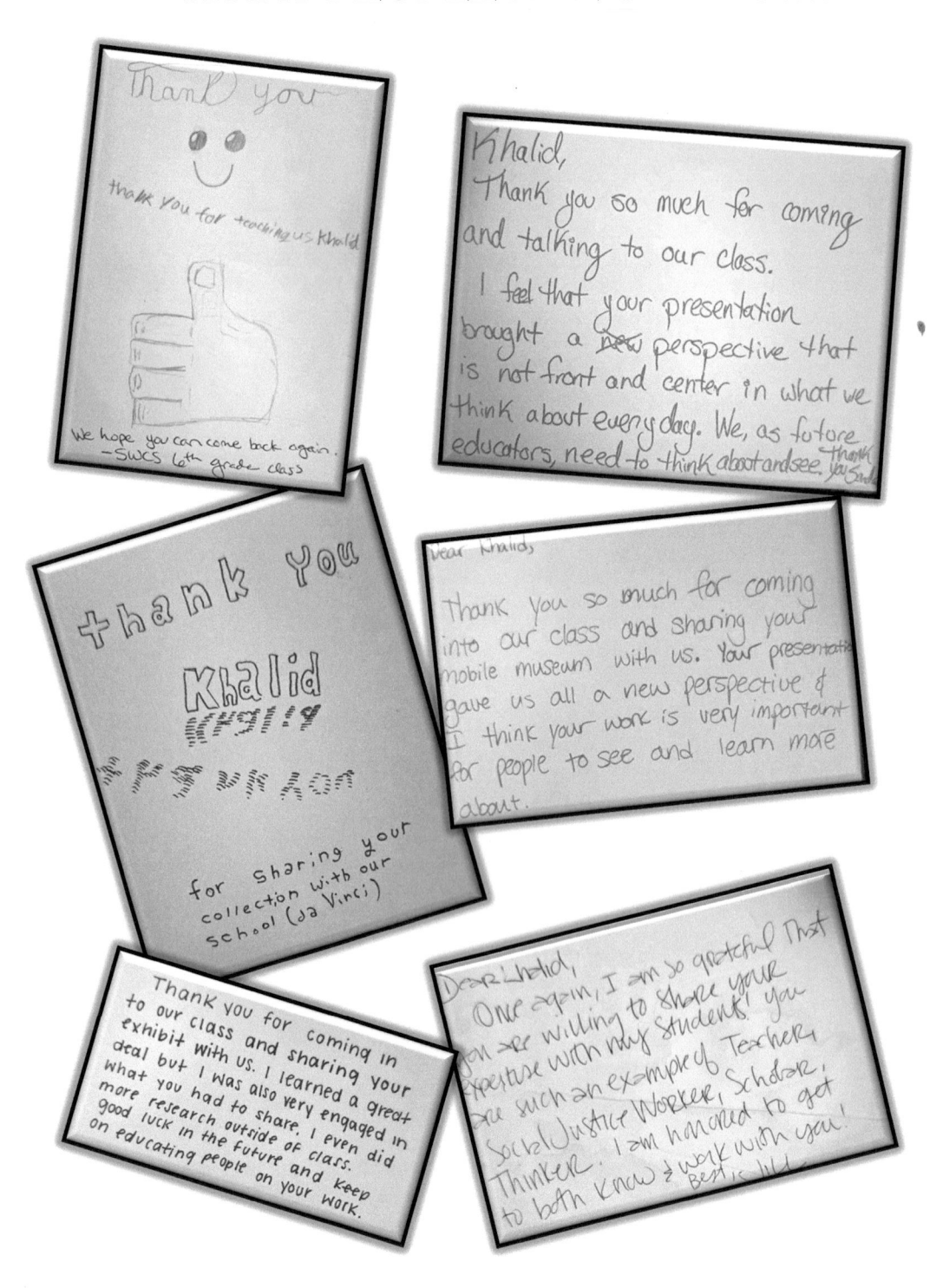

Thank you

thank you for teaching us Khalid

We hope you can come back again.
-SWCS 6th grade class

Khalid,
Thank you so much for coming and talking to our class.
I feel that your presentation brought a new perspective that is not front and center in what we think about every day. We, as future educators, need to think about and see. Thank you Sarah

---

thank you Khalid Kelly Wilson

for sharing your collection with our school (da Vinci)

Dear Khalid,
Thank you so much for coming into our class and sharing your mobile museum with us. Your presentation gave us all a new perspective & I think your work is very important for people to see and learn more about.

Thank you for coming in to our class and sharing your exhibit with us. I learned a great deal but I was also very engaged in what you had to share. I even did more research outside of class. Good luck in the future and keep on educating people on your work.

Dear Khalid,
Once again, I am so grateful that you are willing to share your expertise with my students! You are such an example of Teacher, Social Justice Worker, Scholar, Thinker. I am honored to get to both know & work with you!
Best, Jill

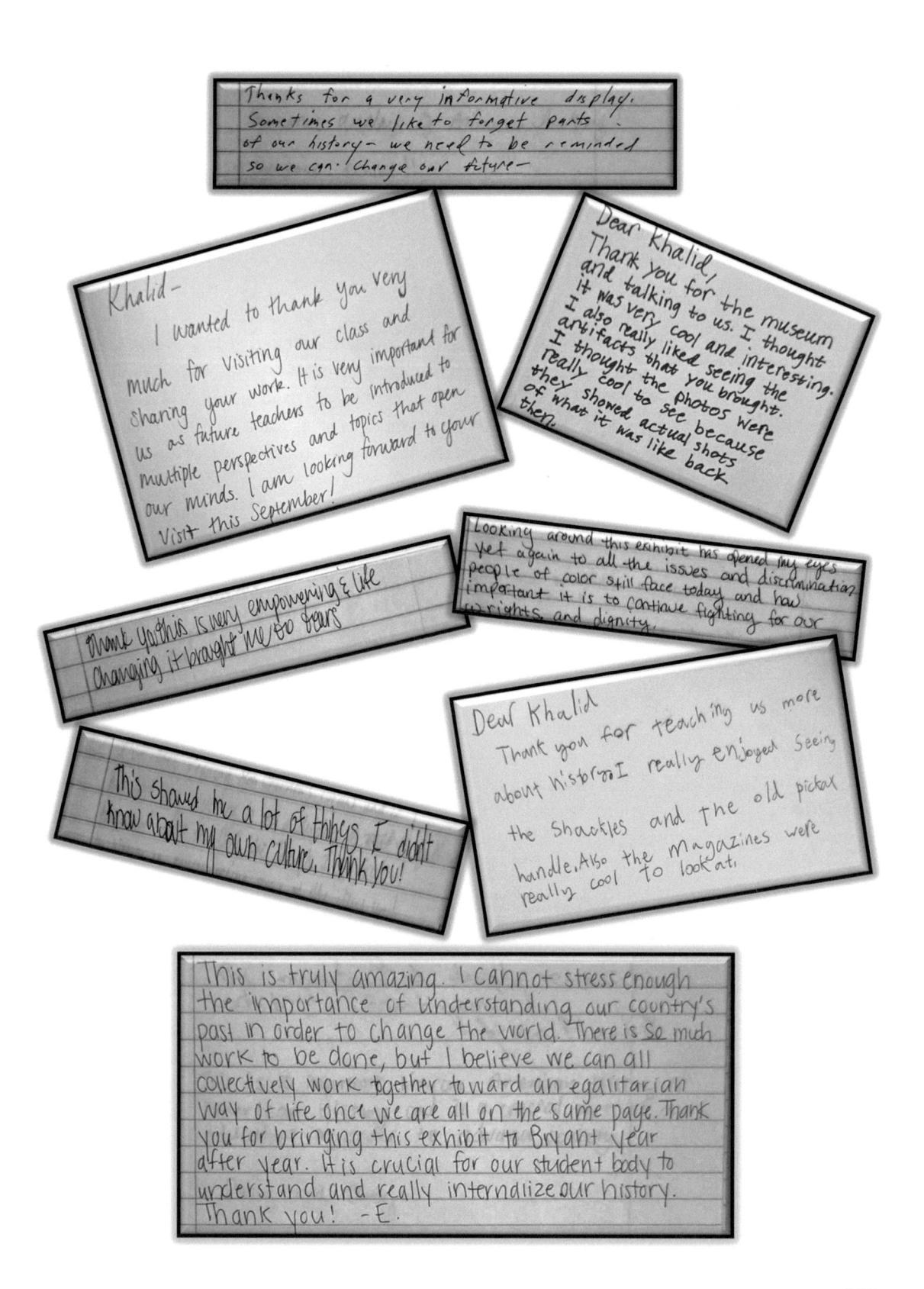

> Thanks for a very informative display. Sometimes we like to forget parts of our history — we need to be reminded so we can change our future.

> Khalid —
> I wanted to thank you very much for visiting our class and sharing your work. It is very important for us as future teachers to be introduced to multiple perspectives and topics that open our minds. I am looking forward to your visit this September!

> Dear Khalid,
> Thank you for the museum and talking to us. I thought it was very cool and interesting. I also really liked seeing the artifacts that you brought. I thought the photos were really cool to see because they showed actual shots of what it was like back then.

> Thank you this is very empowering & life changing, it brought me to tears.

> Looking around this exhibit has opened my eyes yet again to all the issues and discrimination people of color still face today and how important it is to continue fighting for our rights and dignity.

> This showed me a lot of things I didn't know about my own culture. Thank you!

> Dear Khalid
> Thank you for teaching us more about history. I really enjoyed seeing the shackles and the old pickax handle. Also the magazines were really cool to look at.

> This is truly amazing. I cannot stress enough the importance of understanding our country's past in order to change the world. There is so much work to be done, but I believe we can all collectively work together toward an egalitarian way of life once we are all on the same page. Thank you for bringing this exhibit to Bryant year after year. It is crucial for our student body to understand and really internalize our history. Thank you! —E.

Epilogue: Looking forward

As I reflect on the 30th anniversary of the Black History 101 Mobile Museum, I am filled with gratitude, urgency, and resolve. What began as a personal collection of artifacts has grown into a movement, traveling the country to tell the untold stories of Black history, culture, and resilience. This journey has been as much about preserving the past as it has been about inspiring the future. But today, we stand at a crossroads, where the teaching of Black history is under direct attack.

The stakes are monumental. If we do not teach Black history, we risk losing a cornerstone of our collective identity—not just as Black Americans, but as a nation. As James Baldwin once said, *"If you know whence you came, there are absolutely no limitations to where you can go."* To deny Black history is to deny the fuel that powers our resistance, our creativity, and our progress. It is to sever the roots of a tree that has weathered centuries of storms but continues to grow.

The attacks on Black history are not just academic; they are ideological. When states legislate against teaching about slavery, systemic racism, and Black contributions to this nation, they seek to erase the truth. They aim to create a version of America that is sanitized and incomplete. What is at stake is not just the erasure of Black suffering, but also the erasure of Black brilliance, Black innovation, and Black resistance. Without Black history, we lose Harriet Tubman's courage, Malcolm X's clarity, and Fannie Lou Hamer's resolve. We lose the lessons of the Harlem Hellfighters, marching home from World War I, and the vision of Frederick Douglass, who declared, *"It is easier to build strong children than to repair broken men."*

The Black History 101 Mobile Museum will continue its mission, moving forward as an archive, carrying the spirit of Sankofa: going back to fetch what is at risk of being forgotten. But as we look to the future, I am turning my energy toward the **Black Seed Legacy Project**, a vision that aligns with the work of the museum but takes it a step further. Over the next five to ten years, this project will focus on creating and supporting community archives across the country. Black communities hold the keys to their own histories—through family heirlooms, oral traditions, church records, and photographs. The Black Seed Legacy Project will plant the seeds for these community-driven archives, ensuring that Black history is preserved not just in museums but in the hearts of neighborhoods and families.

Marcus Garvey taught us, *"A people without the knowledge of their past history, origin, and culture is like a tree without roots."* The Black Seed Legacy Project is about fortifying those roots. It is about empowering communities to tell their own stories, to own their narratives, and to pass them down to future generations. In a time when history is being weaponized, this project is our shield and our sword.

To all who have supported the Black History 101 Mobile Museum over these 30 years, I say thank you. This work would not be possible without the students, educators, community leaders, and everyday people who see the value in truth-telling. The road ahead will not be easy, but it is necessary. As Audre Lorde reminded us, *"When we speak, we are afraid our words will not be heard or welcomed. But when we are silent, we are still afraid. So it is better to speak."* The Black History 101 Mobile Museum will keep moving. The Black Seed Legacy Project will grow. Together, we will continue to make history—by preserving it, teaching it, and living it. The story is not over; it is only just beginning.

The Black Seed Legacy Foundation is a non-profit organization committed to preserving and sharing the rich history and culture of the African American experience. Our foundation is inspired by the renowned Black History 101 Mobile Museum founded by Dr. Khalid el-Hakim, which has been traveling to communities across the country for the past 20 years, educating and enlightening people of all ages about the Black experience in America.

The Black History 101 Mobile Museum has a distinguished track record of successful exhibits in diverse spaces, ranging from K-12 schools to major corporations. Its extensive archive of over 10,000 artifacts provides a comprehensive portrayal of the African American journey. Now, the Black Seed Legacy Foundation, in collaboration with Dr. Khalid el-Hakim, aims to expand access to this remarkable collection.

Our primary objective is to "seed" select communities with 150 artifacts from the Black History 101 Mobile Museum. These artifacts will serve as a foundation for community archives, ensuring that local history is properly preserved and celebrated. We believe in the power of grassroots efforts and community engagement, so we encourage each community to contribute to the growth of their local archive by adding their own historical artifacts and narratives.

Moreover, accessibility is a core value of the Black Seed Legacy Foundation. We strive to make the archive available to as many people as possible, just as the Black History 101 Mobile Museum has done through its traveling exhibits. We will work closely with communities to develop strategies and partnerships that ensure the archive remains accessible to schools, organizations, and individuals.

The Black Seed Legacy Foundation invites communities across the country to join us in this transformative endeavor. By planting the seeds of knowledge and understanding through the dissemination of historical artifacts, we aim to empower individuals, foster a deeper appreciation for African American history, and contribute to a more inclusive society. Together, we can cultivate a legacy of respect, appreciation, and unity.

For more information contact:
Dr. Khalid el-Hakim
Bhistory101@yahoo.com or 313-645-4197

Made in the USA
Columbia, SC
31 March 2025